YORK NOTES

General Editors: Professor A.N. Jeffares (University of Stirling) & Professor Suheil ~~~~~ University of Beirut)

John Osborne

LOOK BACK IN ANGER

Notes by Gareth Griffiths

BA PHD (WALES)
Senior Lecturer, Macquarie University, New South Wales

LONGMAN
YORK PRESS

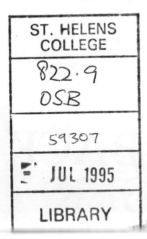
Extracts from *Look Back in Anger* by John Osborne are reprinted by kind
permission of Faber and Faber Ltd, London, © 1957 by John Osborne;
and in the USA by kind permission of S. G. Philips, Inc., New York,
© 1957 by S. G. Philips, Inc.

YORK PRESS
Immeuble Esseily, Place Riad Solh, Beirut.

LONGMAN GROUP UK LIMITED
Longman House, Burnt Mill, Harlow,
Essex CM20 2JE, England
and Associated Companies throughout the world.

© Librairie du Liban 1981

First published 1981
Reprinted 1988 (twice)

ISBN 0-582-02278-9

Produced by Longman Group (FE) Ltd
Printed in Hong Kong

Contents

Part 1

Introduction

Life of the author

The details of John Osborne's life have been examined with great interest by critics because of the feeling that his plays, notably *Look Back in Anger*, have a strongly autobiographical flavour. This is, perhaps, the result of the great stress laid in this, as in many of the subsequent plays, on the protagonist, whose speeches, because of their powerful rhetoric, are often read as 'statements' by the playwright. But any view of Osborne which sees Jimmy Porter as a mouthpiece for the author's own views is an over-simplification. The details of Osborne's life serve only to stress that he was qualified by birth and by his occupations before his success as a playwright to write with sensitivity and insight into the life of the new, déclassé* young figures of the post-war period. His father was a white-collar, middle-class man who married a barmaid. John Osborne himself seems, like many of his contemporaries who wrote about the working class, to have been poised in that no-man's-land which contemporary sociologists have classified as lower-middle class. He was born in 1929. His upbringing was suburban, with hints of a struggle at maintaining a shabby respectability. His educational background reinforces this. He was sent to a third-rate public school, where he declares he was very unhappy. Some of the feelings of dislocation and confusion that we feel in characters like Jimmy, and in characters such as Maitland in his later play *Inadmissible Evidence* (1965),† seem to draw on an effort to be placed effectively in a social system which retains social distinctions, but which has lost the certainty of how much meaning these distinctions still possess. In this sense Osborne's background qualified him to understand the sense of drifting and uncertainty which characterised the period of the early fifties, and drew him into sympathy with characters whose sense of themselves was at variance with the roles they were called upon to play in their society and time. Even when his central figures are historical, as for

---

* Déclassé is a term used by sociologists to indicate people who, as a result of rapid social changes, no longer feel able to identify themselves with any particular social class.

† In which the increasing estrangement from his profession and his social role felt by the leading character, the solicitor Maitland, is reflected in his inability to distinguish the 'real' and the 'fantasy' worlds he inhabits.

example, Luther, in the play of the same name, the characters he selects are ones whose roles involve a crisis of identity based, at least in part, on being called by their intellect or education to fulfil roles which are contradicted by their sense of social inferiority or doubt. Osborne's career before his success as a writer displays this same lack of certainty. He left school early and worked for a couple of years as a journalist on trade papers. Drifting into acting under the old system, where the actor was trained on the job, he spent a number of years as a self-admitted unsuccessful actor in obscure provincial repertory companies.

Osborne says that he never took himself seriously as an actor and that this opinion was shared by others, but he appears to have been competent enough to have secured a number of small parts at the Royal Court Theatre. The significance of this period of his life lay in the experience of the stage as a craft which it afforded him, an experience which may well have been part of the reason for the success his first major play enjoyed.

When George Devine and others sought to create a stage company which would serve to encourage the growth of a modern playwright's theatre they were at a loss for writers. For the opening season they turned to established overseas playwrights and to novelists who were willing to try their hand in the new field. Thus *Look Back in Anger* was mounted in an opening repertoire which included a play by the American Arthur Miller (*b.*1915), already an established figure of the New York theatre, a new play by the novelist Angus Wilson (*b.*1913) which had been premiered 'out of town'* at Bristol and which was well if not enthusiastically received, and a play by the then much acclaimed verse dramatist Ronald Duncan (*b.*1914). Of all these writers only Osborne was an unknown. His play had been submitted in response to a newspaper advertisement requesting plays from new, young writers. In a seminar at the University of East Anglia a number of years ago the novelist Angus Wilson recalled his impressions of Osborne, whose play was being rehearsed at the same time as Wilson's own work *The Mulberry Bush*. 'Osborne was the only one of us all,' Wilson said, 'who had any experience of the theatre. If the director objected to something in my play all I could do was acquiesce. But John would say, well, yes, but why can't you bring him in this way or why can't you do something else. The difference between us was that he knew what could be done on a stage and I didn't. That was where his experience as an actor was so important.'

A little later, and this is recorded from memory, Wilson added that he had always felt that the figures in *Look Back in Anger*, despite the

---

* A phrase referring to the practice of trying out plays in provincial cities, such as Birmingham, Bristol or Oxford, before risking them in London. 'Town' here is London, the theatrical as well as national capital of England.

social origins and characteristics ascribed to them in the play, were really rather strongly reminiscent of the members of a provincial repertory company. Helena, we recall, *is* an actress in the play. But the exuberance and extravagance of Jimmy's language and gestures, and the detached but intellectual stance he adopts lends credence to Angus Wilson's feeling that Osborne's experience as an actor in the provinces is being drawn upon here to flesh out a character and situation.

Wilson's comments are interesting because they point to a quality in Osborne's work which accounts for the attention and praise it received even from many of the critics who did not feel that it was effective in structure, or did not approve of its subject matter and characters. Nearly all the reviewers of the first production comment on the dramatic quality of the play. With all its flaws and all its short-comings it *is* essentially a play, conceived in terms of theatrical perform-ance, and not, like many of the pieces of the period, an adaptation into theatre of ideas conceived essentially in terms of another genre, poetry or narrative fiction. Philip Hope-Wallace's review in *The Guardian* sums up the feeling that many reviewers appear to have had when he ended his notice by saying that:

> Tony Richardson's production and a good set by Alan Tagg help out this strongly felt but rather muddled first drama. But I believe they have got a potential playwright at last, all the same.

Critics have tended in recent years to stress the fact that the revolution-ary effect of *Look Back in Anger* was the result of the exciting and inno-vative subject and characters it explores and not in any way a revolution in form or structure. While this is essentially true it is worth remember-ing that there were many writers who had the capacity to put the situ-ations and people Osborne employs into literature. He had the added advantage that he conceived their presentation and executed it in terms inseparable from its realisation in a theatre, as a play. Above all he was a dramatist, and it was in the bringing together of this commitment to theatre with his commitment in a social sense that the new dynamism lay.

Osborne's earlier work

Look Back in Anger was not Osborne's first play. He had written, and even had productions of, plays earlier. As early as 1950, when Osborne was twenty, a play written in collaboration with Stella Linden called *The Devil Inside Him* had received a brief showing at Huddersfield. Again, the year before his success with *Look Back In Anger*, a play written with Anthony Creighton called *Personal Enemy* was staged at Harrogate. *The Devil Inside Him* was apparently revived at the Pembroke Theatre, Croydon, in 1962 as '*Cry for Love*, by Robert Owen', but the event passed with little notice from the critics and general public. More interesting is the fact that two of the established plays from the later canon were written wholly or in part before the success of *Look Back in Anger*; these were to emerge later as *Epitaph for George Dillon* (again in collaboration with Anthony Creighton) and *The World of Paul Slickey*, Osborne's first attempt at a musical play. These facts give the lie to the idea that Osborne burst on to the scene as an unknown with his first play and became an overnight success. Such dramatic events are part of the new wave in theatre; for example, this is a fair description of what happened in the case of the young Salford girl Shelagh Delaney. Her play, *A Taste of Honey*, was her first attempt at playwriting, inspired, as she has said, by her seeing a Terence Rattigan play and feeling that she could write something better and more truthful. Shelagh Delaney is the reality of the myth which has been associated with Osborne, in that she was a working-class writer who did see her work as bringing a direct and simple statement of the reality of her time into the theatre in 'a plain, unvarnished tale'. Osborne, as his association with the theatre and his early apprentice works show, had a much more general and long-lasting commitment to the theatre and to the task of the playwright. Significantly, Shelagh Delaney's later works have not had the success of her first, and she has ceased to be a major influence on the stage, whilst Osborne's work, despite subsequent failures and even disasters, has developed and changed as he has established the canon of a major dramatist of our time. Whatever else Osborne's work is it cannot be dismissed as merely an interesting sociological phenomenon; for better or for worse each of the plays is the work of a serious and dedicated playwright.

This introduction has stressed Osborne's development as a writer, rather than examining his significance as a representative figure of his time. Much of the contemporary reaction to *Look Back in Anger* when it was first produced has tended to obscure our sense of the play as one whose dramatic qualities, characterisation and linguistic subtleties have allowed it to survive its own time and still speak effectively to us today. But it would be foolish to deny either the importance of the new style of character and event the play treats in establishing itself in its time, or the continuing value the play has in holding up an accurate mirror to the shifts in feeling and attitude that characterised Britain in the early fifties.

Osborne and his time

Many critics and commentators have drawn attention to the way in which Osborne has been labelled as one of the new wave of 'angry young men'. Figures such as Colin Wilson (*b*.1931), Kingsley Amis (*b*.1922) and John Wain (*b*.1925), whose work was lumped together by journalists who detected in it a shared distaste for 'Establishment'* values and a disillusionment with contemporary political life, were in reality quite different in their approach and attitude, as their subsequent developments have shown. But they were certainly linked in being the figures who gave voice to a general feeling of disenchantment which was undeniable by the mid-fifties. Some people have traced this feeling back to the sense of disappointment which followed the failure of the Labour governments of the post-war period to make any significant change in the social and political fabric of life. Certainly, by the beginning of the 1950s there was a desperate air of concern about the decline in Britain's position in the world, its economic depression, and its loss of an imperial presence overseas. There is an air of desperation in the frantic hailing of the new queen's coronation as the beginning of a new Elizabethan Age; the conquest of Everest, significantly by a New Zealander and a Sherpa, was inflated by the media, who seemed desperately to be searching for the kind of certitude in public and private values that more properly belonged to the period of a Scott† than a Hillary**. Later, the Duke of Edinburgh's Award Schemes‡; the Queen's Awards

*The 'Establishment' is a short-hand, journalistic way of referring to the complex of groups, social and political, who hold power in England. Establishment values are therefore those that buttress the existing social institutions which maintain the status quo. To be anti-Establishment is to be at odds with the traditional power bases in society and to be on the side of social reform.

†Captain Robert Falcon Scott, RN (1868–1912), commander of the British Antarctic Expedition of 1910. This ill-fated expedition sought to discover the South Pole, and ended in the deaths of the Polar party when returning from the Pole to their winter base. The tragedy was compounded by the fact that they had been beaten to the Pole by the Norwegian explorer Amundsen, who had reached it a few days earlier. The gallantry and self-sacrifice displayed by Scott and his men, recorded in their diaries and journals, became a symbol of personal gallantry to which British people aspired as an ideal. Such idealism was soon to be eroded by the social conditions of the Western Front in the 1914–18 war.

**Sir Edmund Hillary (*b*.1919), a New Zealand writer, lecturer and mountaineer. Together with the Sherpa guide Tenzing he was the first man to reach the summit of Mount Everest in May 1953. News of the successful British Everest Expedition came at the time of the Coronation of Elizabeth II. The press hailed the climb as proof that the spirit of confidence and expansiveness which characterised the reign of the first Queen Elizabeth in the sixteenth and seventeenth centuries and which was a high-point of English history and culture would return under the new young queen. Needless to say the prophecy was not fulfilled.

‡These were schemes initiated by the Queen's husband, Philip, Duke of Edinburgh, to encourage young people to participate in their society and to engage in 'character-building' activities. Much of the philosophy of the scheme was a revival of the traditional 'healthy mind in a healthy body' ideal of the English public school, and great stress was laid on outdoor activities; but the schemes also involved projects of help for the aged, the disabled and the needy.

to Industry, The 'I'm Backing Britain' movement*, all in their varying ways excellent and worthy ideas, fall together into a pattern symptomatic of a nation searching to confirm an assurance in ideals and moral standards which it suspects has been lost. The national consciousness is indeed looking back in this period, as it struggles to recover a confidence which it associates with the periods of its past greatness. The advantage of hindsight allows us to see that although Osborne was hailed as an iconoclast and 'a self-pitying, self-dramatising intellectual rebel' he was, in fact, very much a child of his time, since his work shares this backward-looking, nostalgic longing for a past which offered stable values.

In addition Osborne is a child of his time in the way in which his work looks forward to the spirit of protest expressed by later movements such as CND† and articulated in books such as Jeff Nuttall's *Bomb Culture*. Underlying all these phenomena is the feeling that only a *moral* protest is possible in a world where political parties and national power groups have become the victims of a massive technological complex which has robbed them of any convincing identity. A new world picture is coming into focus, a picture in which only identical monolithic power blocks can be discerned. These blocks are capable of aggressive imperialism, and of violence. This violence erupted in such events as the suppression of the Hungarian uprising and the invasion by France and Britain of the Suez Canal zone, both of which occurred in the year Osborne's play was written. It is this spirit, as yet inarticulate and buried, that Jimmy Porter can be seen to be groping towards when he denounces as products of 'the American Age' the attitudes and ideas of his time. For Jimmy Porter the kind of cohesive view necessary to a movement is not yet possible. He is still stunned by the process of

---

*This was a scheme to encourage new confidence and support for British workers, and to foster the buying of British-made goods in preference to foreign manufactured items. It began when some office workers decided to work additional hours without extra pay as their personal contribution to the revival of the British economy. From this beginning it spread and became a campaign to restore pride in British achievements and British manufacturing. Its sign, which for a while was seen in many shops, restaurants and factories, was the Union Jack flag with the superimposed slogan 'I'm Backing Britain'. The movement quickly lost impetus and died away as rapidly as it had begun.

†The Campaign for Nuclear Disarmament was a mass movement to protest against the possession of an independent nuclear deterrent by Britain and against the presence of NATO nuclear strike forces on British soil. It was strongest in the late 1950s and early 1960s. It united many people from different walks of life and of different classes, people who would otherwise have had little in common at a political or social level. The annual highlight of the movement was the Easter March to the nuclear base at Aldermaston. Thousands of ordinary people joined left-wing politicians, liberal churchmen, academics and students in this mass demonstration. The Campaign was not successful in obtaining its goal and gradually lost its impetus, ceasing to be a force in British political life by the mid-1960s.

betrayal which has destroyed the possibility of the kind of commitment he associates with his father, and with the political idealism of the 1930s. His accurate sense of the irrelevance and futility of such idealism in his own time, a time when 'there are no good brave causes left', leaves him unable to do anything positive himself about the political situation. But his denunciation is a superb reflection of the disillusion and anger which fed the responses of the next decade. Jimmy Porter is a character who expresses Osborne's sense of his time as a period of transition. When he wrote *Look Back in Anger* it seems clear that Osborne had little idea of what the future held, but the play is redolent of his sense of the impossibility of a culture standing still. It is this innate sense of energy as the ultimate and inescapable product of human suffering and human struggle that the play portrays so brilliantly.

The theatre of the time

Much of the success of *Look Back in Anger* in its own time must be related to the stagnant and unexciting nature of the English theatre in the post-war period. There had been very little fundamental change in the style of plays which the public had been offered since the 1930s. Indeed, as critics have noted, the leading dramatist of the day, Terence Rattigan (1911–77), had had his first major success as early as 1936. There had been an attempt at innovation in the work of the verse-dramatists, notably Christopher Fry (*b*.1907), Ronald Duncan (*b*.1914), and, not least, the poet T.S. Eliot (1888–1965). They had sought to revitalise drama by bringing it back to poetry. But the language they employed although poetic was essentially non-dramatic. It was language which sought to verbalise rather than create action on the stage. It lacked physical quality of the poetry of the Elizabethan plays, and finally remained poetry *in* the theatre rather than poetry *of* the theatre, concerned with description divorced from enactment. With the exception of this one brave movement in verse drama the theatre, especially the commercial Shaftesbury Avenue theatre which dominated the immediate post-war scene, was content to revive classics and to produce a string of imitative social documentaries of middle-class life and drawing-room comedies.

Overseas plays had not remained stagnant. The best of the American theatre in this period was shown in the plays of such writers as Tennessee Williams (*b*.1914) and Arthur Miller (*b*.1915), but their work was expressing a social and cultural reality too far removed from the English condition to serve as an effective model. The experimental work in Europe, especially in France, and to a lesser extent in Germany, had been noted by some people working in English theatre. But the influence of this work was slow to make itself felt. The two outstanding

indicators of changes to come in the early 1950s were the production by
Peter Hall of Samuel Beckett's* *Waiting for Godot* at the Arts Theatre,
London, in 1955; and the visit to England of Brecht's East German
Company, the Berliner Ensemble† in 1952. The most immediate result
was in the fillip such things gave to individuals and groups, encouraging
them to set up companies whose financial and artistic aims would provide a counterbalance to the narrow, commercial perspectives of the
Shaftesbury Avenue managements. Two major influential companies
arose from this impetus: the Theatre Workshop of Joan Littlewood,**
which she established at the Theatre Royal, Stratford East, in a working-
class suburb of London's East End, and which sought to bring theatre to
the people and help young playwrights to learn their craft in a workshop
atmosphere; and the English Stage Company which George Devine
(1910–66) established with the financial and moral support of the great
patron Lord Harewood, which also sought to develop performance
expertise in a repertoire whose primary aim would be to encourage and
foster the development of new contemporary works. It was this company which established itself just off the West End in the Royal Court
Theatre at Sloane Square. The choice of theatre was a happy one, since
it had been the Royal Court, which had served as the venue for the very

* Samuel Beckett (*b.*1906), author and playwright, was born in Dublin, Ireland. After a
career as a university lecturer in French he moved to Paris where he became a protégé of
the Irish expatriate writer James Joyce. Beckett has written a series of complex novels and
a number of plays, of which *Waiting for Godot* (1953) was the first and, perhaps, remains
the most successful. Beckett's themes are loneliness, isolation and suffering. His characters reflect a world in which belief in universals is increasingly difficult and in which man
is left alone without a sustaining faith to help him to endure the difficulties of life.
† Bertolt Brecht (1898–1956) a German playwright and theatre director whose Marxist
beliefs led him to a rejection of the existing naturalist theatre. To Brecht theatre meant a
commitment to the task of changing society. Theatre was a tool to help people to see more
clearly the social forces which were shaping their lives. To this end he exposed the workings of his theatre, demanding that the spectator remain fully aware of the fact that he was
watching a play, unable to lose himself in the illusion that he had entered another world.
An exile from Germany during the period of the National Socialists, he returned to East
Germany in the late 1940s and founded a company to put his ideals into practice and to
mount productions of his own plays. This company, known as The Berliner Ensemble,
helped to spread Brecht's practices and ideals both before and after his early death in 1956.
** Joan Littlewood has worked with various street-theatre groups since the early 1930s,
presenting plays in public places in an effort to take theatre out to the people. During the
Second World War she was banned for her political views, which were considered too
radically left. Neither the BBC nor the Forces' entertainment organisation, ENSA, would
allow her to work with them. In 1945 she founded the Theatre Workshop and in 1953 this
group settled at the Old Theatre Royal at Stratford East in the largely working-class East
End of London where they performed a mixed repertoire of adapted classics and new
works. Working as an ensemble, that is, with permanent actors and writers discussing
works as they were being mounted, the Theatre Workshop produced some of the most
lively plays of the post-war period. In 1975 Joan Littlewood left England to work in
France. She has been one of the most influential figures in contemporary English theatre.

influential Barker-Vedrenne seasons* of 1904–7, the seasons in which Shaw had been established as a writer in the eyes of the general public.

The growth of these new companies provided an outlet, for the first time, for writers to have their work considered by managements prepared to take a risk on new plays, and, in the case of Joan Littlewood particularly, to work with writers in the process of learning the craft of making a play. The new plays which resulted not only proved the existence of a body of writing talent able to respond to this new possibility, but also showed that there was an audience for theatre that the commercial managements had failed to satisfy. This audience of young people had, at least in part, grown up in a new age, the television age. For them any theatre that was going to succeed would at least have to offer an insight into their lives as powerful and immediate as they had come to expect from the best television documentary and drama. For them 'the magic of the theatre' was a hackneyed phrase. Even at its worst television was capable of producing an immediacy of involvement and a directness of response to shifting habits and ways of life which allowed this audience to identify with situations familiar to it. It was with such an audience, possessing these kinds of expectations, that the new companies were learning to communicate. Significantly, much of the financial success of *Look Back in Anger* was attributable to television, when an act of the first production was shown on the television screen. The instant rise in ticket sales confirmed the link that the next decade was again to confirm between the new audience for theatre and television. In its turn the new work that emerged from the companies formed in the mid-1950s fed back into television, with directors such as Lindsay Anderson (*b*.1923) whose involvement with the new social drama spilled over into an involvement with documentary and with television's potentiality to show the social problems and issues of the time. In the same way in drama the television play reflected the way in which the possibilities for an immediate and truthful presentation of social conditions, expressed by dramatists such as Osborne, Wesker and Delaney, could be effectively developed by a medium which could take its cameras into the world and record fact side by side with fiction.

---

* During the years 1904–7 the theatrical entrepreneur J.J. Vedrenne (1867–1930) obtained the services of the young director Harley Granville-Barker (1877–1946) to present a season of Shakespeare and other classics at the Royal Court Theatre and later at the Savoy. Barker's direction was revolutionary, and, in addition, he persuaded Vedrenne to allow him to mount some matinée performances of Bernard Shaw's *Candida*. These were so successful that finally, of the thirty-two plays presented during the seasons, eleven were by Shaw, accounting for no less than 701 of the 988 performances given. In other words Shaw, arguably the most influential playwright of the century in England, was established as a commercial success by these revolutionary seasons.

Conclusion

Look Back in Anger should be judged as a play written in a time and place ready and willing, because of a number of factors, to see itself in fresh ways. But it can also legitimately be viewed as a play whose purpose was essentially theatrical, that is to portray a man's response to his time through presentation of the interaction of character and event. In this sense the play is open to be judged as a play which may still speak to us some twenty or more years later. Its initial success was founded on the fact that it seemed to articulate the buried responses of its own day; its continuing success will depend on how far we judge its perception of those responses to have incorporated more than just a limited historical view of the human condition.

A note on the text

There has been no alteration or emendation to the text first published in 1957 by Faber, London, issued as a paperback in 1960 and in many subsequent reprints. This was the text used at the first performance of the play, which was given at the Royal Court Theatre, Sloane Square, London, on 8 May 1956, by the English Stage Company. It was directed by Tony Richardson, with decor by Alan Tagg. The players were: Jimmy Porter, Kenneth Haigh; Cliff Lewis, Alan Bates; Alison Porter, Mary Ure; Helena Charles, Helena Hughes; Colonel Redfern, John Welsh.

All page references in these notes are to the Faber paperback edition.

Part 2

Summaries
of LOOK BACK IN ANGER

A general summary

Look Back in Anger concerns a group of young people living in a
Midland town in the mid-1950s. The husband, Jimmy Porter, is an ex-
undergraduate who has married a wife from a class higher than his own.
They share their flat with a young, uneducated friend, Cliff, who helps
Jimmy runs a sweet-stall in which business he has been set up by the
mother of a friend of his, Hugh Tanner. Most of the play is occupied
by the long tirades of abuse which Jimmy heaps on his society, its
absence of values and its hypocrisy. Much of this abuse spills over into
scathing, if bitterly humorous, attacks on his friend and his wife. It is
clear that Jimmy blames her for her origins and cannot find a way to
reconcile the hatred this engenders with the love and attraction for her
which he also feels.

The arrival of Allson's friend Helena causes Alison, who, without
Jimmy knowing, has become pregnant, to decide to leave him. She
returns home with her father, and Jimmy has a brief, unsatisfactory
affair with Helena. In the meantime Alison has lost her baby and when
she returns, broken and in pain, as Jimmy had hoped she would, Helena
leaves to allow them to take up the threads of a relationship which can
survive only by a process of fantasising against the dreadful reality of
their situation. At the end of the play they are left clinging together in
tender and resigned despair.

As John Russell Taylor wrote as early as 1961 in his study of the new
wave of dramatists entitled *Anger and After*, John Osborne's 'revolutionary' play which shocked and puzzled its first audience in 1956 is essentially a 'well-made-play' following the basic three act structure conceived
by the French dramatists Eugène Scribe (1791–1861) and Victorien
Sardou (1831–1908) in the mid-nineteenth century, and developed as
the principal dramatic formula for comedy and 'serious' drama in the
following hundred years.

In its simplest form the 'well-made-play' formula seeks to provide a
logical ordering of events designed to maintain dramatic suspense and
to keep an audience sufficiently informed to be interested but puzzled
enough not to be bored. To this end it divides the play into three major

units: exposition, complication and dénouement (or unravelling). The exposition serves to provide the basic information about plot, character and scene to allow an audience to place the action in its social and geographical context. It introduces the relationships between the major figures, and provides, through dialogue, those facts about their lives and the events they have experienced which are necessary for the audience to be able to understand the situation on the stage. The exposition also allows the dramatist to place some apparently innocent piece of action—a letter, a reference to a meeting, or something similar—which will be used later in the action as a device to resolve the complexities which follow.

Complication (or *scéne à faire*) is the part of the action, usually Act Two, or Acts Two and Three in a four-act structure, where the situation of the exposition is deepened and complicated by new events, the forging of new interactions, or the revelation of the consequences of the past and its effect on the present, often effected by the return of some character from the past.

The third and final stage of the action, the dénouement, allows the solution of the complexities or brings them to a crisis which ends the action of the play. Often the buried devices from the exposition surface here to provide such a resolution.

Clearly *Look Back in Anger* cannot be fitted into this formula as into a mould. But many of its elements are present. Act One, which is long and undivided, does serve to introduce all the major characters either on stage or by description. We meet Jimmy, Alison and Cliff, and are shown the uneasy but functioning relationship they have established. We are introduced to Helena, and are shown the disruptive effect her entrance is likely to produce. We are given lengthy descriptions of all the other characters whose relationships with the main figures in the play shape their present responses. Primarily these are Alison's father and mother; Hugh's mother, who has set Jimmy up with his sweet-stall; Hugh himself; Webster, the only one of Alison's friends whom Jimmy can tolerate, and so on, right down to minor characters, rapidly sketched in the dialogue, such as Alison's brother Nigel.

We learn about Alison's pregnancy, the factor that will come up again in a more complex way in Act Two and which provides a sort of resolution when she loses her child in Act Three. We are introduced to the game of bears and squirrels, the full explanation of the significance of which is held over until Act Two Scene One, when Alison tells Helena how it became 'the one way of escaping from everything' for both of them. Finally, the act ends with Jimmy's receiving the news of the death of Hugh's mother, providing an effective climax and allowing the complication of Act Two, Alison's resolution to go home, to occur in the period of his absence.

In many ways, then, this first act is constructed in a very direct and simple way along the traditional lines of a 'well-made-play'. It provides all the information we need, outlines the characters and their situations and paints a vivid picture of the atmosphere of stifling boredom into which Jimmy's frustration and violence burst like thunder in sultry, heavy weather.

Act Two is subdivided into two scenes. The first scene is concerned primarily with the effect on the existing situation of the arrival of Alison's friend, Helena. Helena is puzzled, appalled and yet intrigued by the situation she finds. At first she functions as a device to allow Alison to tell the audience in greater depth about the early days with Jimmy. In Act One Alison has had to be a silent character. Now, for the first time we are allowed to 'go behind' and see the events of the past from her point of view. In this sense the first section of Act Two Scene One is essentially *expository* (that is, concerned with exposition or providing information).

Helena, as an alternative and fresh target, allows Jimmy to renew his attacks; but in passing we learn of his own past and childhood. Clearly we could not learn this so easily in dialogue between Jimmy and characters he already knew well. Helena, then, in Act One Scene One functions strongly to enhance and develop the exposition, serving as a catalyst to allow strands of the past which bear on the situation presented in Act One to be revealed to us in a greater depth.

Act Two Scene One also begins the process of complicating the action by introducing the potential for future dramatic ironies, for instance, Jimmy's hope that Alison will learn to suffer, to understand the meaning of pain, sets up the potential for their response to the loss of their child in Act Three.

Act Two Scene Two introduces the new figure of Alison's father, an ex-Indian Army colonel. This character serves to complicate the action further by failing to behave in the stereotypical way we might expect. His sympathy for his daughter's plight is modified by his sense of how she may have been partly to blame for the estrangement between herself and Jimmy. A sense of continuity if not similarity between the colonel and Jimmy complicates any simple decision we might be tempted to make in favour of one or other of the characters who have been introduced.

When Helena tells Jimmy at the end of the act that Alison is to have a baby, and he reacts in a violent and bitter outburst, she reveals as the climax of Act Two the attraction she has felt for him and which has emerged only obliquely up until this point. The act ends with their passionate embrace.

The complications established in Acts One and Two are now fully wound up and Act Three must resolve them.

The time passage between Act Two Scene Two and Act Three Scene One is the longest in the play ('several months later'). At first nothing appears to have changed except that Helena is substituted for Alison as the main target of Jimmy's abuse. Her reactions are less profound, and his abuse, as a result, less intense. It is a recapitulation of the main theme of the first act but in a minor key, muted and falling in tone. Actions which are repeated underpin this—for example the ironing board is again involved in a piece of horseplay.

Cliff's leaving emphasises this too, since it is clear that he feels he has lost his role when Alison leaves. There is no real struggle between Jimmy and Helena, and his purpose as a buffer and intermediary has gone. The first scene of this final act ends with the return of Alison. Helena seems almost relieved and resolves the situation by asserting her intention of leaving. Jimmy and Alison are left alone to renew their struggle. But there has been a change. Alison, through the loss of the baby, has arrived at that point of desolation which Jimmy wished for her and she capitulates in the longest and most agonised speech she has in the whole play. At the end, Jimmy and she can only retreat again to the temporary refuge of bears and squirrels, leaving any future apart and in doubt.

Detailed summaries

Act One Scene One

Act One Scene One introduces us to the characters of Jimmy Porter, his wife Alison and their friend Cliff, who share a rented flat in a small Midland town. It is a Sunday afternoon and the season is spring, but here there is no atmosphere of flowers, trees and blue skies, the things usually associated with spring in English writing. Instead we are introduced to a gloomy, claustrophobic atmosphere in which boredom and dull weather combine to create a heavy, dull and stifling mood.

Alison, the wife, is ironing, and the two men are reading the Sunday newspapers. In the dialogue which follows we learn that Jimmy Porter has been educated at one of the new redbrick universities*, but that he has chosen to earn his living by running a sweet-stall, an occupation in

---

* The term 'redbrick university' was used originally to distinguish the new city universities, such as London, Manchester, Liverpool, Leeds and others from the old medieval universities such as Oxford and Cambridge. Jimmy's university is obviously meant to be one of the newer and less well regarded of these city universities, since Alison tells Helena in Act Two Scene One that Jimmy claims his university isn't 'even red-brick but white tile', that is, it is a very recently built institution. This emphasises the fact that Jimmy is one of the new generation of post-war graduates whose education arose from the 1945 British government's expansion of educational opportunities through scholarships and grants.

which he is helped by his friend Cliff, who, unlike Jimmy, has not been to university. Alison, Jimmy's wife, is from a higher social class than Jimmy, and he clearly resents this. In addition we see that there is a great deal of personal antagonism between the two, an antagonism mitigated by the presence of Cliff who acts as a buffer between them.

Very little happens during the scene in the form of direct action. Much of the dialogue is conducted in the form of monologues by Jimmy Porter and these serve to reveal the complexity of his character by the way in which they demonstrate the basic insecurity underlying his surface belligerence. In addition, the reactions of Cliff and Alison show that although they are both targets for Jimmy's abuse they retain a great deal of affection and love for him.

Throughout the opening act Jimmy abuses Alison and Cliff for their lethargy and lack of involvement, abuse which culminates in a long speech with a demand for an enthusiasm which he feels all of them have lost (p.15). A very strong undercurrent of almost sentimental nostalgia for the past counterpoints this abuse. This note of regret at the loss of an assured past is strongly sounded throughout, for instance when the archetypally English music of Vaughan Williams (1872–1958) and the image Jimmy conjures up of the lost assurance of Edwardian England are summed up by the character in a line which encapsulates the sense of loss he feels along with his anger when he contemplates the past: 'If you've no world of your own, it's rather pleasant to regret the passing of someone else's (p.17).'

Much of Jimmy's abuse is directed at Alison's family, and reflects the deep class divisions of England in the 1950s, and Jimmy's sense of not being able to find himself a place in society to which he can feel he belongs. Throughout this section the social attack on Alison is combined with a deep resentment which Jimmy clearly feels for women, seen as the symbol for an acceptance of things as they are which he cannot tolerate. During the battles between Jimmy and Alison, Cliff acts as a sounding-board and a restraint on the excesses of Jimmy's outbursts. This role culminates when the mock struggle between them causes an accident in which Alison's arm is burnt (p.26). Jimmy's subsequent regret again underlines the real love he feels for Alison, inadequate and impractical though it is.

Towards the end of the act a new character is introduced as we learn that Helena Charles, a friend of Alison's, is coming to stay (p.37). This provokes the most violent attack of all from Jimmy, and the act culminates in his curse-like outburst in which he wishes that Alison might be exposed to suffering, so that she could learn how to become a 'recognisable human being'. The heart of this speech is his desire that Alison might conceive and lose a child, so that she should be exposed to an experience she could not dismiss or put aside.

NOTES AND GLOSSARY:

the White Woman's Burden: this remark ironically compares Alison's resigned and yet superior stance as she irons throughout Jimmy's tirades to the attitude of the British to the natives during the colonial period. The reference is to Rudyard Kipling's poem 'The White Man's Burden' (1896)

And Mrs Porter gets 'em all going with the first yawn: again an ironic comparison of Alison's attitude to that of T.S. Eliot's Mrs Porter. In this case the allusion includes Alison's mother, and the implied training her daughter has received from her, since the reference is to *The Waste Land* (ll.199–201), which runs: 'O the moon shone bright on Mrs Porter/And on her daughter/They wash their feet in soda water.' The final image, of course, stresses the waste and extravagance of the middle classes, and their indulgence of themselves

You'll end up in the *News of the World*, boyo: the *News of the World* is a well-known English scandal sheet, renowned for printing stories of adulteries, illicit love-affairs, rapes etc. The term 'boyo' is Anglo-Welsh, and is, perhaps, best translated as 'mate' or 'friend'. In the context it has a slightly jocular tone

the mass meeting of a certain American evangelist at Earl's Court?: Earl's Court is a large stadium in London, and the reference is to the fashion in Britain in the 1950s for the holding of prayer meetings conducted by visiting American evangelists such as Billy Graham, in which people were 'converted' in an atmosphere of mass-hysteria

Priestley's piece: J.B. Priestley, the novelist and playwright, wrote a weekly newspaper column in the 1940s and 1950s, dispensing a mildly nostalgic and 'down-to-earth' form of liberal Socialism

the Edwardian twilight: the Edwardian period, between the turn of the century and the outbreak of the First World War, can be viewed as the transitional period between the assured attitude of Victorian England and the excesses of total war, which swept away the last vestiges of nineteenth-century confidence. Hence the concept of a twilight period between the high day of Victorian confidence and the coming night of twentieth-century doubt and scepticism

Vaughan Williams: an English composer who drew heavily on English folk-music for his themes. Hence in the context Jimmy's interest in his music suggests his profound 'Englishness' and his deep involvement in the traditions of English culture

Proper little Marchbanks: this refers to the ineffective poet in *Candida*, a play by George Bernard Shaw (1856–1950), whom Candida trails behind her as a lover, and whom she uses to blackmail and threaten her husband. In the context it suggests that Cliff is being ironic about the real relationship between Jimmy and his older lover, Madeline

Ulysses: Odysseus, the Greek hero, whose voyages, described in Homer's *Odyssey*, culminated in his sailing out of the known world through the Pillars of Hercules in search of a new world. The image is clearly one Jimmy would like to have of himself. There is, perhaps, a buried irony in the fact that Penelope, wife of Ulysses, is the mythic epitome of long-suffering patience and faithfulness

A sort of female Emily Brontë: Emily Brontë was, of course, a woman, and a famous nineteenth-century novelist. Jimmy reverses the sex because, as we later discover, Webster is a homosexual

the Marquess of Queensberry manner: Douglas Williams, fourth Marquess of Queensberry (1724–1810), was a famous sporting peer who drew up the first rules to regulate the sport of boxing. The implied point is that Alison's mother appears to play by the rules by her polite manner but that beneath this surface she remains a vicious and unscrupulous opponent

The Lady Pusillanimons . . . Behold the Lady Pusillanimons: the whole section here draws on the metaphor of the Roman Games to describe again the vicious and depraved reality which Jimmy insists exists beneath the polite and cultivated surface of English middle-class society. The reference is picked up by Cliff (p.28): 'I'm wondering how much longer I can go on watching you two tear the insides out of each other.' This is a line in which the image implies that Jimmy and Alison are like two gladiators or wild beasts in an arena, locked in mortal combat. The image appears in a submerged form in many places in the play

Miss Drury: it is possible that a slight buried reference exists here to the famous, traditional and hide-bound theatre in Drury Lane. Osborne's play has a number of these buried literary references through names, for example Hugh Tanner and Mrs Tanner may well suggest the hero of Shaw's play *Man and Superman* (1903), John Tanner, author of the supposed *Revolutionist's Handbook*. Significantly, Jimmy has adopted Mrs Tanner as his surrogate mother, suggesting a parallel between himself and John Tanner

a Morris Dance: a form of traditional English dance which has been revived. Originally a peasant dance, it is usually now danced by people who seek, perhaps, self-consciously, to recover the old traditions. Hence Jimmy's comment, 'Let go my foot, you whimsy little half-wit.' Notice how Cliff has touched on a sore point with Jimmy in the preceding line: 'You're a stinking old bear, you hear me?' This draws attention to the whimsical and selfconscious game which Alison and Jimmy use to escape the reality of their own condition, the game of squirrels and bears in which Jimmy is cast as the bear

expense of spirit: this refers to Shakespeare's Sonnet No. 129. The full couplet runs: 'Th'expense of spirit in a waste of shame/Is lust in action '

Old Gide: this refers to the French novelist André Gide (1869–1951), who was homosexual

the Greek Chorus boys: again this refers to the fact that the Greeks practised homosexuality as a 'higher' form of love than heterosexual love

He's like a man with a strawberry mark: the man with the strawberry mark was Oedipus, whose birthmark in *Oedipus Rex*, by the Athenian dramatist Sophocles (496–406BC), revealed him as the man who had killed his father and lain with his mother. Hence Jimmy is referring to Webster's homosexuality as a secret shame which he keeps thrusting into people's awareness as a means of insisting on his identity

the Michelangelo Brigade: Michelangelo Buonarroti (1475–1564), an Italian painter, sculptor, architect and poet, was acclaimed from early youth as a great artist and enjoyed the patronage of several leading Italian statesmen, notably the ruler of Florence, Lorenzo de Medici, and Pope Julius II. Although perhaps not quite such a universal genius as Leonardo da Vinci, his great contemporary, Michelangelo created masterpieces in many fields of the arts. His best-known works include his statue of the young David in Florence, the painted roof of the Sistine Chapel in Rome and the great basilica, St Peter's, in the same city. Michelangelo never married and it has often been supposed that he was homosexually inclined. The evidence, although not conclusive, is generally accepted by most critics and commentators

All the references here serve two purposes. First, they establish that Jimmy is rejecting women. He is not homosexual; the speech makes this quite clear; but he is pointing to the second issue, that is that women and domesticity, children and social responsibilities often stifle creativity. Therefore many homosexuals have been deeply creative, since they are not so burdened. It is an extreme form of the battle between the sexes which the references to Shaw's *Man and Superman* also underline, since in that play the struggle between John Tanner and Ann Whitfield is a struggle between man's desire to create artistically and to dare new things and women's desire to hold and nurture what exists, protecting the biological life-force on which the continuance of the species depends

playing with the company at the Hippodrome this week: 'The Hippodrome' is a typical name for a small provincial repertory theatre of the period, the kind of theatre Osborne would have have been very familiar with from his own period as an actor, producing solid and safe established plays in a traditional style

---

Act Two Scene One

The first scene of Act Two takes place two weeks later in the same setting. Helena has arrived and is staying as a guest. The scene opens with a long conversation between her and Alison in which Alison describes to Helena, and so, obliquely, to us, the way in which she and Jimmy met, the opposition of her parents to their relationship, and the subsequent events when she and Jimmy began to live together. Helena is clearly trying to understand the complex situation in which she finds herself, a situation she has never encountered before, and which appals and yet fascinates her. Thus, for example, she tries (p.41) to probe the affectionate and yet non-sexual relationship which exists between Cliff and Alison.

The curiosity of Helena serves as a device to allow Alison to tell the audience details of her courtship with Jimmy. Thus we learn of the 'raids' which Jimmy and his friend Hugh Tanner conducted on the middle-class homes of Alison's parents' friends, 'raids' in which they gate-crashed* parties and imposed themselves on the polite society they despised (pp.43–5). Alison describes her own complicated reaction to this process, a fascination not unlike that which Helena also clearly feels at the present time. She points out (in the long speech on p.45) that the opposition of her parents to the relationship crystallised her own strong feelings for Jimmy, and made up her mind to marry him.

The long conversation with Helena is also used to allow Alison to tell the audience about the game of squirrels and bears which she and Jimmy play to escape the intolerable strains and contradictions of their relationship (p.47). Cliff's entry after this speech serves to link the conversation with the first encounter of Jimmy and Helena that we have been shown (p.48). In the dialogue which follows Jimmy turns the attack from Alison to Helena, renewing his abuse of the middle class in general and Alison's family in particular, now that he has a fresh audience (or target). Jimmy's long diatribe against Helena modifies into a series of speeches (pp.57–8) in which he tells her, and us, the background to his own life. In particular he describes the relationship between his parents, and the effect on him of the experience of watching his father die as a result of the privations he had suffered in the International Brigade in the Spanish Civil War (July 1936–May 1939).

This speech is interrupted when Jimmy becomes aware that Alison is really going to church with Helena, as she had said she was (p.51). He views this as a complete betrayal, though as yet there has been no clear sign that Alison is contemplating leaving him for good and returning to her parents. Provoked by this 'betrayal', he launches into a violent attack on Alison, reminiscent of the attack at the end of the first act (p.59). It is interrupted by a telephone call, and Jimmy leaves Cliff alone with the two women. In the most significant speech he has in the play (p.60) Cliff explains to Helena and, perhaps, to Alison too, what his role has been in the relationship. Using Alison's confusion Helena tells her that she has sent a telegram to her father telling him to come and take Alison home. Alison, pregnant and tired, capitulates.

* Gate-crashing is the art of arriving at a party to which one has not been invited. Jimmy and Hugh are deliberately flouting social conventions in order to shame Alison's parents and their friends.

When Jimmy returns with the news that Hugh's mother is dying Alison is too exhausted to react and allows Helena to lead her off to church, leaving Jimmy, who wants her to go with him to Mrs Tanner's death-bed, alone and in despair.

NOTES AND GLOSSARY:

at the flat in Poplar: many of the local names in the play have special social and class connotations for a British audience. The reference to Poplar, a working-class suburb of London, reinforces Alison's comment in the speech which follows and emphasises that she has dropped out of one world into another

We'd set out from headquarters in Poplar, and carry out raids on the enemy in W.1, S.W.1, S.W.3 and W.8: the same process occurs here. The postal codes are of areas in London where wealthy and successful people live

Sometimes I thought he might even dress the part—you know, furs, spiked helmet, sword: this implicitly compares the raids by Jimmy and Hugh on the cocktail parties with the Viking raids on Saxon England (c AD856–1035). There is an edge of sarcasm implied here

the New Millennium: this refers to the traditional concept that the world would change entirely when the first thousand years of history after Christ had passed, and to the belief that this would coincide with the Second Coming of Christ. It became an idiomatic way in Western culture of describing a Utopian vision of a future in which all things would be perfect and just. Again, Alison's tone here is ironic

fey: magical, but in context used to imply slightly self-conscious and whimsical

discussing sex as if it were the Art of Fugue: *The Art of Fugue* is a collection of pieces by Johann Sebastian Bach (1685-1750), a German musician whose work is intricate and usually associated with the mastery of very complex musical forms, such as fugue. Hence the reference to his work here. Bach's music is not congenial to a romantic such as Jimmy

The Cess Pool: Jimmy likes to make literary references. Here he is showing off his knowledge by punning on the title of T.S. Eliot's famous poem *The Waste Land* (1922)

this saint in Dior's clothing: parodies the traditional phrase, 'a wolf in sheep's clothing'. Christian Dior (1905-57) was a world-famous and expensive Paris couturier

Pass Lady Bracknell the cucumber sandwiches, will you?: this refers to a character in *The Importance of Being Earnest* (1895) by Oscar Wilde (1854-1900), and again implies Jimmy's distaste for the pretensions of polite society. Cucumber sandwiches are a traditional part of upper-middle-class teas

I suppose you're going over ... it's a capital gain and it's all yours: this long section seems to draw heavily on the Musical Banks section from Samuel Butler's *Erewhon* (1872). Butler (1835-1902) was an evolutionary theorist, social satirist and novelist who influenced many people, among them George Bernard Shaw. *Erewhon* is a satirical novel set in an imaginary country; its traveller-hero describes the strange institutions he finds there, implicitly satirising Victorian English social institutions. The Erewhonian banking system is a satire on the Church: piety is invested for a dividend of salvation

the war in Spain: the Spanish Civil War followed the election of a left-wing Republican government in Spain in 1935. The conservative forces led by General Franco revolted and a bloody civil war ensued. Many left-wing sympathisers from other countries went to Spain to fight in an International Brigade on the Republican side. The Republic was defeated. Jimmy's father was obviously one of these people. In many ways the Spanish Civil War was the last great romantic crusade of the twentieth century, though it was marked by bitterness, internal division and a sense of betrayal by the left of the left. It is to this that Jimmy is in part referring when he says that there 'are no good, brave causes left'

You Judas!: Judas was the disciple who betrayed Christ to the Romans and the Sanhedrin (Council of the Jews) for thirty pieces of silver. He is now the archetype of all traitors and betrayers

I'm not the District Commissioner, you know.: the District Commissioner was a colonial official who governed a territory during the days of the British Empire. One of his duties, as depicted in fiction and legend, was to keep the peace between warring native tribes. See, for example, *Sanders of the River* (1908) by Edgar Wallace (1875-1932) or the various African novels of Joyce Cary (1888-1957)

Act Two Scene Two

This is a short but important scene, since it deepens our understanding of the character of Alison. It opens with Colonel Redfern, Alison's father, having arrived to take her home. The conversation between them is interesting since it reveals that Colonel Redfern has a much deeper understanding of the situation than we might have expected. Colonel Redfern is shown to have a sense of the similarity between Alison and himself, a sense of the way in which they both have a tendency 'to sit on the fence because it's comfortable and more peaceful'. He has been unable to stand up to Alison's mother. Alison, he implies, might have made a difference in her marriage if she had been able to give Jimmy the unqualified loyalty he demanded.

The long reverie of the colonel (pp.67–8) shows the same nostalgia for the past that colours some of Jimmy's speeches (pp.67–9). There is a psychological base for the sympathy which is implied between them. Alison sums it up when she says:

'You're hurt because everything is changed. Jimmy is hurt because everything is the same. And neither of you can face it. Something's gone wrong somewhere, hasn't it . . .' (p.68)

The moment of decision for Alison comes immediately after this and is rendered through action, not through dialogue. When she picks up the squirrel, looks at it, then puts it back rather than into her suitcase, she is consciously rejecting the only possible route other than her leaving. Significantly, Helena, we learn, is staying. Her reason is clearly an excuse. With Cliff's entry the tone shifts again, and Alison clearly shows the love she still has for Jimmy by her concern for him. After Alison and Colonel Redfern leave, the conversation between Cliff and Helena clearly shows that Cliff grasps Helena's double interest in getting Alison to leave. As he goes out he thrusts the letter at her, remarking

'You give it to him. [*Crossing to the door*] He's all yours. [*At door*] And I hope he rams it up your nostrils.' (p.71)

This letter is one of those devices so necessary in a naturalist play to focus the audience's attention in dialogue which can reveal inner states only tentatively because of the need to maintain a surface illusion of 'reality'. It passes from Alison, to Cliff, to Helena. And so it shows the inability of Alison or Cliff to encounter Jimmy at this time. When Helena picks up the bear and looks at it, she reinforces our sense that Cliff is right, and that she does have an interest in Jimmy herself.

When Jimmy enters he is bitter and violently angry, but also deeply hurt. Helena tells him that Alison is pregnant. The outburst which follows again stresses the vulnerability of Jimmy underneath the violence. When Helena slaps him, and draws him down to her, it is in an image in which her passion is mingled with a maternal solicitude.

NOTES AND GLOSSARY:

A Charwoman who married an actor: a charwoman is a cleaning-woman. The term implies a working-class woman. Significantly the two elements of the play, class and theatre, are drawn together in the description of this secondary character

A good blow-out . . . : idiomatic expression, meaning a good meal or a good feast

That is the famous American question—you know, the sixty-four dollar one: this refers to an American quiz show popular in Britain in the 1950s in which the winning question was called the 'sixty-four dollar question'

Shelley . . . Godwin: The references here to Shelley, Mary and William Godwin refer to Percy Bysshe Shelley, the poet (1792–1822), to his writer wife Mary Wollstonecraft Godwin (1791–1851), daughter of the rational philosopher William Godwin (1756–1836). The parallel implies that Alison feels that Jimmy cannot come to terms with what she and her father really are, or what he is, and has to cast them in roles too complex for them to sustain. It also implies her awareness that, as we have seen from the evidence of his speeches, Jimmy lives his life as if it were a literal re-enactment of his education, constantly seeking parallels between his experience and the unattainable ideals he has absorbed from literature and art

came back in '47: Colonel Redfern would have returned from India in 1947 since India was granted independence and became a republic in 1948

the Blimps: Colonel Blimp was a famous cartoon character who summed up all the jingoistic elements of the retired Indian Army officer. The term became a general one for all those who could not come to terms with the decline of Britain as an imperial force, and who regarded the past glory of the Empire as the only reality in a changing world. It implies a blind attachment to the values of the past and a refusal to view the present in any light but that of deteriorating standards

Act Three Scene One

The third act opens in a situation almost exactly parallel with the opening of Act One, except, of course, that Helena now occupies the role that Alison played in the opening. Jimmy and Cliff bicker over the Sunday newspapers, and Jimmy keeps up a running commentary which shows his fascination with, and yet hatred of, the intellectual apparatus of the society he despises. The new element in the attack which follows is the stress on the religious observance which Helena has sustained, despite Jimmy's influence. Failing to provoke a satisfactory response from Helena by pointing out to her that she is 'living in sin' (p.78), Jimmy and Cliff begin a routine which draws heavily upon the techniques of the music-hall stage and combines these techniques with literary references. It is almost as if Jimmy is seeking to create an image of a form of art in which the two poles of his personality can meet; his deep and nostalgic attachment to the popular traditions of England, and his brittle, sophisticated twentieth-century consciousness which tells him that the world which sustained these truly popular forms has disappeared in the anonymity of 'the American Age' (pp.80–2). A struggle ensues between Jimmy and Cliff (p.82) which parallels the struggle in Act One. Significantly, although Helena is ironing, in this act she does not get burned. The implication is that she is not as involved as Alison, and that everything which is happening is only a pale shadow of the real events of Act One. Cliff feels this and remarks to Jimmy, comparing Helena to Alison, 'It's not the same, is it?' Jimmy's denial lacks conviction:

> JIMMY: (*irritably*) No, of course it's not the same, you idiot! It never is! Today's meal is always different from yesterday's and the last woman isn't the same as the one before. If you can't accept that, you're going to be pretty unhappy, my boy. (p.83)

At this point Cliff announces his decision to leave. The reasons he gives are clearly to cover his real motive, which is his sense of purposelessness. Since there is no real struggle between Jimmy and Helena there is no real reason for a friend to act as intermediary. Jimmy's response links his sense of loss at Cliff's leaving to his sense of there being no 'good brave causes left'. And the alternative he sees is to be 'butchered by the women' (pp.84–5). The intellectual desolation Jimmy embodies has spilled over into his personal life, and we become aware of the extent to which he was as dependent on Alison as she was on him.

This despair is clearly what motivates Jimmy in the final conversation with Helena when, empty and purposeless, or as he puts it 'heartily sick of the whole campaign, tired out, hungry and dry' (p.86), he allows himself a sentimental and romantic dream '. . . I'll close that damned sweet-stall, and we'll start everything from scratch. What do you say? We'll get away from this place' (p.86). Helena's acquiescence, 'I say that's wonderful', is interrupted by the entry of Alison, untidy and ill. Jimmy leaves, leaving the two women alone.

NOTES AND GLOSSARY:

an evil orgy in Market Harborough: the long section here centres on the witch cults which were popular in Britain in the 1950s and 1960s, and which were usually a cover for the middle-class to indulge in a little illicit sex spiced with mysticism. The class context of the comment is emphasised by Jimmy's reference to Fortnum and Mason's, an upper-middle-class London store famous for its high-quality prepared foods

down at the Y.W.: Y.W. is short for Y.W.C.A. or Young Women's Christian Association, a hostel for young Christian women

Harrods: as with Fortnum and Mason's, an upper-middle-class London store

. . . pale Cambridge blue: blue blood is traditionally associated with the upper classes. Pale blue is the colour of Cambridge University. The image links the two together

Coptic Goddess of fertility: the Copts were the native population of Egypt from about the third to the tenth century AD. Coptic was a mixture of ancient Egyptian and Greek. The Copts were, according to the early Christian writers such as Eusebius, converted to Christianity by St Mark the Evangelist. The Coptic church still survives to this day. Presumably, Jimmy is referring to the way in which such new Christian ideas as the adulation of the Virgin Mary are in fact simply grafted on to earlier, pagan fertility-goddess rites. The Coptic reference is invoked to suggest the grafting of new traditions on to old. The inadequacy of the image reminds us that neither Jimmy Porter, nor the playwright who created him, is a historian of ideas

Fellow of All Souls: All Souls is an Oxford college which consists almost entirely of elected Fellows. It is one of the traditional sources of political power and patronage within the British academic system

the Athenaeum: a London club whose membership is made up largely of academics, scholars and churchmen

And jocund day stands tiptoed on the mysty mountain tops: from Shakespeare's *Romeo and Juliet*, III.5.9–10; this is the farewell scene between the lovers after they have consummated their secret marriage

T.S. Eliot and Pam: Thomas Stearns Eliot, author of *The Waste Land*, perhaps here symbolises the poetry of modern man, fragmented, desolate and in pain. Pam seems to be a reference to the figure in John Betjeman's (*b*.1906) poem 'Pot Pourrie from a Surrey Garden' (1940): 'Pam, I adore you, Pam you great big mountainous sports girl,/Whizzing them over the net, full of the strength of five,/That old Malvernian brother, you zephyr and khaki shorts girl,/Although he's playing for Woking,/Can't stand up/To your wonderful backhand drive.' Pam, in this context, epitomises a healthy, vigorous, and rather dumb English middle-class girl

little Gidding: an oblique reference to Little Gidding, one of the poems in T.S. Eliot's *Four Quartets* (published as a whole in 1946; first published in different sections, the first in 1936)

Flanagan and Allan: a comic duo, the leading men of the Crazy Gang which ran a famous vaudeville/music hall show at the Palace Theatre, London, for many years through the 1930s and 1940s. They were famous for duets accompanied by a soft-shoe dance routine

Roedean: one of the most famous and expensive of England's public schools for girls

You look like Marlon Brando or something: this refers to the famous scene in the film of *A Streetcar Named Desire* (1947) a play by Tennessee Williams in which Marlon Brando plays the Polish American Stanley Kowalski, who always wears a skivvy or vest, and leans out of the window screaming his wife's name, Stella. This was an image that passed into popular folk-lore in the Fifties

Pinner or Guildford: respectable but dull middle-class dormitory suburbs of London

Please give your blood generously: franks of this type were used in the 1950s as part of the blood donor campaign

Act Three Scene Two

This final scene follows on almost immediately from the preceding one. Throughout the conversation between the two women Jimmy's trumpet can be heard playing jazz very loudly in the room offstage. The difference between Alison and Helena is brought home in the conversation which follows. Helena asserts the continuity in her of a traditional moral belief, which her sexual passion for Jimmy has not altered. Alison, we learn, has lost the child she was to bear. In the conversation between the two women we see the clarity with which each, in her own way, sees Jimmy. But Helena is clearly relieved by Alison's return. She declares her intention of leaving, and her inability to sustain a relationship which demands that she yield up the sanctuary of her traditional concepts and open herself to the flux of modern experience. Alison is also shown as seeing how any single relationship will be insufficient to sustain the kind of openness Jimmy demands. As she says:

'He wants something quite different from us. What it is exactly I don't know—a kind of cross between a mother and a Greek courtesan, a henchwoman, a mixture of Cleopatra and Boswell.' (p.91)

Maddened by the trumpet, Helena calls Jimmy, who enters reluctantly. Helena tells him that she intends to leave.

'. . . I do love you, Jimmy. I shall never love anyone as I have loved you. [*Turns away L.*] But I can't go on. [*Passionately and sincerely*] I can't take part—in all this suffering. I can't.' (p.93)

Jimmy's reaction throughout this scene is low-key. He, too, has clearly felt the loss of the child as he has earlier remarked:

'I don't exactly relish the idea of anyone being ill, or in pain. It was my first child, too, you know. But [*he shrugs*] it isn't my first loss.' (p.92)

Alison's reply, 'It was mine', clearly moves him. Thus, when Helena announces her inability to suffer further, Jimmy's response is pitched from this earlier tone, almost dissociated from her.

JIMMY: [*in a low, resigned voice*] They all want to escape from the pain of being alive. And, most of all, from love.

The church bells, which throughout the play have been symbolically countered by the now silent jazz trumpet, start ringing again. Jimmy's comment is now to Helena:

'It's no good trying to fool yourself about love. You can't fall into it like a soft job, without dirtying up your hands.' (p.93)

Helena leaves and Jimmy and Alison are alone again. It is to the image of the bear that he returns, but now it is significantly related to the experience of the play as a whole:

> 'The heaviest, strongest creatures in the world seem to be the loneliest. Like the old bear, following his own breath in the dark forest. There's no warm pack, no herd to comfort him. That voice that cries out doesn't *have* to be a weakling's, does it?' (p.94)

The despair he feels is now in the open, and his final appeal to Alison is a straightforward and direct one: 'I may be a lost cause, but I thought if you loved me, it needn't matter' (p.95). Her response is the most frank and total commitment she has achieved in the play. Whether for good or bad, as the result of her experience, she is no longer sitting on the fence. Wholeheartedly she joins him in his despair: 'I don't want to be a saint. I want to be a lost cause. I want to be corrupt and futile' (p.95).

In the long speech that follows she bares her soul for the first time, and reveals that she has finally been through the flames of suffering through the loss of the child. For better or for worse, she and Jimmy have arrived at the bottom of the pit: 'Don't you see! I'm in the mud at last! I'm grovelling! I'm crawling! Oh, God . . .' (p.95). Jimmy, distraught and desperate at the very moment he has waited for, when Alison will join him wholly in the personal hell he sees as the essence of modern life, is overwhelmed and cannot stand it: 'Don't. Please don't . . . I can't . . .' (p.96). There is no further place for them to retreat in *reality*. They have joined each other in a personal hell of consciousness, and the only place for them to retreat to is the safety of the fantasy world of bears and squirrels:

> 'We'll be together in our bear's cave, and our squirrel's drey, and we'll live on honey and nuts—lots and lots of nuts. And we'll sing songs about ourselves . . .'. (p.96)

At the end of the play they are together, even if they have nowhere to go.

NOTES AND GLOSSARY:

St Pancras: a London railway station, mainly servicing the Home Counties

the divine rights of marriage . . . constitutional monarchy: the metaphor implied here refers to the period of English history when the Stuart dynasty of the early seventeenth century asserted that the King ruled by divine right. It was opposed by the growing power of the English parliament. A civil war followed which the parliamentary forces won. The Stuart King Charles I was tried and executed, and a Protectorate replaced the monarchy under the leadership of Oliver Cromwell. In 1660 the monarchy was restored but the intervening period had left its mark, and henceforth the power of the king was limited by the power of the people, expressing itself through Parliament. From this point we can date the beginning of the modern British system of constitutional monarchy. The parallel that is being drawn is between the traditional and modern concepts of the rights of monarchy and the traditional and modern views of the rights of marriage

an Eminent Victorian: this refers to the title of Lytton Strachey's (1880–1932) famous collection of biographical essays, *Eminent Victorians* (1918). The irony of Alison's applying this to Jimmy is that it shows us that she is clearly aware that his demand for a pure and 'virile' moral response is at least as much the hangover of the past in his makeup as it is his response to the present. His mourning of the passing of the good brave causes in the previous scene underlines the truth of this

one of the Renaissance popes: the Renaissance popes were renowned for their worldliness, the splendour of their courts, their interests in the secular as well as the spiritual world, and their tendency to ignore the rules of clerical celibacy

a mixture of Cleopatra and Boswell: Cleopatra was the famous Queen of Egypt who seduced, successively, Pompey, Caesar and Mark Anthony. She is a symbol for sexual attraction and potency. James Boswell (1740–95) was the amanuensis and recorder of the words and deeds of the eighteenth-century writer and commentator Dr Samuel Johnson (1709–84). The paradox implies that Jimmy needs something almost impossible for any single woman to achieve, and certainly beyond the scope of the middle-class girls to whom he is drawn by his own insecurity and desire for revenge

I'm in the fire and I'm burning: images of hell and purgatory appear quite frequently in the play. Here they culminate in an image of the lake of fire traditionally supposed to be the abode of the devil, his fallen angels and lost souls of the damned

Part 3

Commentary

Introduction

Look Back in Anger is often dismissed even now as a play which has dated and the interest of which is purely historical. Usually this view of the play accompanies an interpretation which suggests that there is only one properly realised central character: Jimmy. It further suggests that the other characters are ineffectively drawn, and serve only to fill out the gaps in Jimmy's series of dramatic monologues.

Let us consider the implications of this view, and try to look at the text of the play to see if it is borne out by the evidence or not.

Jimmy: characterisation

A good place to begin might be the characterisation of Jimmy. Osborne is clearly in the tradition of English dramatists beginning with Bernard Shaw, and descending through J.B. Priestly (*b*.1894), Somerset Maugham (1874–1965) and Terrence Rattigan (1911–77) who offer a very detailed account of their characters and the situations they are placed in through stage directions. Look at the detailed and complex description offered in the opening stage direction (pp.9–10) of Jimmy Porter's character:

> *. . . we find that* JIMMY *is a tall, thin young man about twenty-five, wearing a very worn tweed jacket and flannels. Clouds of smoke fill the room from the pipe he is smoking. He is a disconcerting mixture of sincerity and cheerful malice, of tenderness and freebooting* cruelty, restless, importunate, full of pride, a combination which alienates the sensitive and insensitive alike. Blistering honesty, or apparent honesty, like his, makes few friends. To many he may seem sensitive to the point of vulgarity. To others, he is simply a loudmouth. To be as vehement as he is is to be almost non-committal.*

Clearly, if this description of Jimmy is realised in and through the

---

* Freebooters were pirates licensed by the government to attack enemy ships, a practice widely followed in the Anglo-Dutch naval wars of the seventeenth and eighteenth centuries, and in the Anglo-French wars of the late eighteenth and early nineteenth centuries. The term has come to mean an irregular soldier who fights on his own terms and not entirely under the discipline of the country he supports.

dialogue which follows, that is, if the actor who plays Jimmy is given the opportunity by the text to reveal the full complexity of the description, then it will be impossible to dismiss Jimmy Porter as 'a mere mouthpiece', or even a 'spokesman for his generation'. The description draws attention to the paradoxical nature of Jimmy—tenderness and cruelty, cheerful malice, and so forth.

Osborne appears to be inviting us here to consider the character of Jimmy in a complex way. He is instructing the actor who plays the part to search the character for its hidden possibilities. There is a stress on the weakness and unsureness of Jimmy, a strong hint that the verbal force and energy is the product of a nervous tension within the character, and is in contradiction to his physical appearance. He does not have a strong physical appearance: he is 'a tall, thin young man'. He smokes a pipe, which he uses as a device to assert a masculinity and assurance that perhaps, in reality, he does not possess. He is a character, the description suggests, who has a strong need to compensate on the surface for weaknesses within himself, weaknesses which he perceives, but not too well or too completely. As a result, there is a feeling behind the description that there are possibilities latent in Jimmy for the capturing of the audience's sympathy if they perceive the real figure behind the mask, the unsure, tender and honest young man behind the blustering, cruel and arrogant surface.

Most people, reading or seeing the play for the first time, would find this a difficult task. The reaction of the reviewers of the early performances has been typical of that of many members of the audience at later performances of the play. Here, for instance, are the views of Patrick Gibbs, reviewing the first production of the play in 1956 for the *Daily Telegraph*:

> The leading character, a man of education living in poverty, would seem to be intended as a full-length study in resentment. Something of a sadist and very much an exhibitionist, he has married above himself, apparently out of spite against middle-class respectability. His wife he lashes with a verbal fury that is often witty and always cruel. It is not, however, resentment that is personified as much as self-pity and this causes the sympathy, which the author intends, to be withdrawn. When his wife left him, it seemed she was fortunate. When she returned to him in the end, a broken spirit, were we intended to cheer?

What these comments draw attention to is the immediate focus of sympathy in the first act on Alison and her plight, a focus which is aided by the sympathetic presentation of Cliff. The result of this is to throw into sharp relief those elements in Jimmy Porter's character that Osborne describes as 'freebooting cruelty' and to play down those aspects of his character which reveal the tenderness beneath. Certainly

in the opening few minutes of the play we would be forgiven for failing
to register the tenderness of Jimmy at all. Instead we should probably
note the picking, nagging insistence with which he goads his wife and
his friend:

JIMMY: I've just read three whole columns on the English Novel. Half
of it in French. Do the Sunday papers make *you* feel ignorant?
CLIFF: Not 'arf.
JIMMY: Well, you *are* ignorant. You're just a peasant. [*To Alison*]
What about you? You're not a peasant are you?
ALISON: [*absently*] What's that?
JIMMY: I said do the papers make you feel you're not so brilliant
after all?
ALISON: Oh—I haven't read them yet.
JIMMY: I didn't ask you that. I said—
CLIFF: Leave the poor girlie alone. She's busy.
JIMMY: Well, she can talk, can't she? You can talk, can't you? You
can express an opinion. Or does the White Woman's Burden make it
impossible to think? (pp.10–11)

Yet the atmosphere of the opening helps to establish some legitimacy
to Jimmy's claim that the other two are stifling him, and themselves.
The slow opening, with only the occasional sound of Alison's iron, the
rustling of the papers, the long, boring emptiness of a chilly, spring
evening captures the mood in a small Midland town where there is
nothing to do, and nowhere to go, except the pictures or the pub.

In addition, despite Jimmy's nagging aggression, there are subtle
indications to the audience that Jimmy's cruelty is part of a complex
defence mechanism which hides his own basic insecurity. Notice how
careful he is to sprinkle his attacks on the 'posh Sundays' with enough
intellectual references and word games to prove his right and ability to
be critical of them: 'the English Novel'; 'the White Woman's Burden';
and, in an ironic allusion to T.S. Eliot's Mrs Porter (in *The Waste Land*)
'And Mrs Porter gets them all going with the first yawn.'

On the surface Cliff's tenderness towards Alison may appear to
emphasise Jimmy's aggression and cruelty. But Cliff shows affection
and understanding towards Jimmy too, and the audience is required
to notice his tone, and modify their response as a result. Thus, when
Cliff kicks out at Jimmy in Alison's defence, there is instantly a note of
comic tenderness in his following comment, as if he is trying to tell
Jimmy that he understands and that he is buffer for them both, not just
for one alone.

CLIFF: [*leaning forward*] Listen—I'm trying to better myself. Let me
get on with it, you big, horrible man. Give it me. [*Puts out his hand
for the paper*]

It is Cliff who draws our attention to the most overt clue to Jimmy's insecurity and weakness, in his joking attack on his need for food.

JIMMY: [*picks up a weekly*] I'm getting hungry.

ALISON: Oh no, not already!

CLIFF: He's a bloody pig.

JIMMY: I'm not a pig. I just like food—that's all.

CLIFF: Like it! You're like a sexual maniac—only with you it's food. You'll end up in the *News of the World*, boyo, you wait. James Porter, aged twenty-five, was bound over last week after pleading guilty to interfering with a small cabbage and two tins of beans on his way home from the Builder's Arms. The accused said he hadn't been feeling well for some time, and had been having blackouts. He asked for his good record as an air-raid warden, second class, to be taken into account.

JIMMY: [*Grins*] Oh yes, yes, yes. I like to eat. I'd like to live, too. Do you mind?   (p.12)

Jimmy's response to Cliff (notice that he grins) indicates an appreciation of the imagination in Cliff's story, and is a clue to the attraction that has drawn them together as friends. He is also tacitly acknowledging Cliff's role as helpmate to both of them. But behind this psychological exchange there is Cliff's perception that Jimmy is like a child, whose eating is a cry for comfort in a world where he is always falling down and cutting himself on the edges of things.

In response to the play's opening it would be easy, ignoring such signs, to dismiss Jimmy Porter as just another 'Rebel Without A Cause', a self-indulgent young man who doesn't know what he wants and screams and shouts because he can't get it. Much of his behaviour conforms with this childish pattern, for instance his screaming at Alison to make tea (p.12), and then his sudden announcement that he doesn't want any (p.14). Jimmy Porter does behave through much of the opening act, where the audience is experiencing his character for the first time, like a spoilt child. He wants the moon. But beneath the self-indulgence, the small hints in the text are sufficient for an actor with skill to indicate that this is a symptom rather than the root of his character. Restless, selfish and egotistic as his responses are, they are nevertheless rooted in a legitimate anger against a world where people make no demands, but are content to accept what they are offered. His anger is directed at those who come close enough to be struck, but his dissatisfaction is with himself, and with his inability to change the world. At his best in this scene he does not escape his own denunciation:

JIMMY: Oh heavens, how I long for a little ordinary human enthusiasm. Just enthusiasm that's all. I want to hear a warm thrilling voice cry out Hallelujah! [*He bangs his breast theatrically*] Hallelujah! I'm alive! I've an idea. Why don't we have a little game? Let's pretend that we're human beings, and that we're actually alive. Just for a while. What do you say? Let's pretend we're human.

Although the attack here is directed dramatically towards Alison, the shift from first person singular to first person plural indicates that Jimmy is including himself in his condemnation. It is interesting to speculate what the other actors might do at a moment like this. Cliff, perhaps, would look away, in a moment of embarrassed perception. Hence his next line ('What did he say?'); Alison, perhaps, allows her eyes to rest on the bear and squirrel on the sideboard, the nearest she and Jimmy get to 'being human'.

The insight behind this speech is picked up in an amplified way in Osborne's later play *The Entertainer* (1957), when the fading stage comic, Archie Rice, reflects on an old black jazz singer he heard sing years ago in America:

... She was poor and lonely and oppressed like nobody you've ever known. Or me, for that matter. I never even liked that kind of music but to see that old black whore singing her heart out to the whole world, you knew somehow in your heart that it didn't really matter how much you kick people, the real people, how much you despise them, if they can stand up and make a pure, just a natural noise like that, there's nothing wrong with them, only with everybody else ... But you won't hear it anywhere now. I don't suppose we'll ever hear it again. There's nobody who can feel that. I wish to God I could ...

In *The Entertainer* Archie Rice expresses his own sense of failure, and of personal involvement in the process, much more clearly than Jimmy Porter. But behind Jimmy's attacks is the same half-formed sense of his own collusion in the process of conformity and acceptance which he despises. To miss this note in the character is to miss the subtlety of Osborne's conception of this complex figure.

The fact that Jimmy Porter's protest is mingled with nauseous self-pity and self-indulgence ought not to swamp our awareness that he is crying out in genuine anguish, and that the source of this anguish is in his awareness, as in Archie Rice's, that he too is finally passionless, convictionless and adrift, unable to act because of his own sloth and inadequacy:

'Nobody thinks, nobody cares. No beliefs, no convictions and no enthusiasms. Just another Sunday evening.' (p.17)

Or, as Archie Rice later expresses the same feeling:

'I wish to God I were that old bag. I'd stand up and shake my great bosom up and down, and lift up my head and make the most beautiful fuss in the world. Dear God, I would. But I'll never do it. I don't give a damn about anything, not even women or draught Bass.'

(The Entertainer, pp.70-1)

It is, of course, still legitimate to ask what it is that Jimmy Porter wants, and to direct critical attention to the fact that he himself has no really clear idea of what that is. In fact he has no really positive future aim at all. In the present his cry is always for something to happen, anything! If happiness, love, certitude and moral security seem unattainable, then he will settle for opposition, argument, hatred and mutual destruction. Jimmy Porter abhors a vacuum, since in nothingness he is faced with an image of his own emptiness and desolation. Jimmy's response to Webster makes this demand clear. Webster stands for everything Jimmy hates, in an abstract way, but he is a worthy opponent, and as Jimmy says,

'. . . When he comes here, I begin to feel exhilarated. He doesn't like me, but he gives me something, which is more than I get from most people.'   (p.18)

In the absence of an enemy, what is left except to tear to pieces the people you love, and ultimately yourself?

Jimmy's involvement with the past

The essential point about Jimmy's character and his role in the play is his relationship with the past. The title, *Look Back in Anger*, contains the essential contradiction which the character of Jimmy explores. He is angry when he looks back at a past in which he longs to be contained, but which he cannot ever quite accept. This is not because he has a better ideal or dream to offer, but because he cannot accept the dreams of the past except by a process of sentimentalising them. At the heart of the character seems to be an anger at being cast-off and excluded. And in this mood he is as capable of sentimental idealism as anyone in the play. It is not surprising therefore that he should have a kind of grudging respect for Alison's father, Colonel Redfern. Like Redfern, Jimmy survives by idealising the past, and by creating defensive pockets of memory to which he can retire when the emptiness of his present and the desolation of his future become too much to bear.

Each of his past relationships is treated in this fashion, that with Madeline, for instance. Jimmy's account of Madeline is clearly presented as a rejection of the present in terms of the past so that it involves us in the process of evaluating Jimmy's responses through the reactions of Cliff and Alison, the central though often neglected technique of much of the action of the play. Alison picks up the reference before Jimmy can bring it out into the open. Her response is clearly one of resignation, tinged with bitterness born of the sense that she can never replace these images Jimmy defends with a selective memory:

> JIMMY: . . . he gives me something, which is more than I get from most people. Not since . . .
> ALISON: Yes, we know. Not since you were living with Madeline. [*She folds some of the clothes she has already ironed, and crosses to the bed with them*]
> CLIFF: [*behind paper again*] Who's Madeline?
> ALISON: Oh, wake up, dear. You've heard about Madeline enough times. She was his mistress. Remember? When he was fourteen or was it thirteen?
> JIMMY: Eighteen.
> ALISON: He owes just about everything to Madeline. (p.18)

Cliff's response to this exchange, one in which Alison takes over the directing of the flow of conversation for the first time, also reveals the way in which Cliff hides a good deal of his real reaction, a process to which we are given a clue by the buried literary reference to Shaw in his next reponse:

> CLIFF: I get mixed up with all your women. Was she the one all those years older than you?
> JIMMY: Ten years.
> CLIFF: Proper little Marchbanks, you are.*

Jimmy's reaction to this indicates the sense in which he is taking the response of the other two. For the first time in the play he hovers on the defensive, since the reaction he has provoked is almost one of resigned boredom. His stories have been heard before. Like Colonel Redfern hovering on the brink of nostalgia, Jimmy is repeating the well-worn anecdotes of an idealised past. Cliff seeks to change the subject by talking about the sweet-stall. But Jimmy is unable to suppress the anecdote:

> JIMMY: . . . She had more animation in her little finger than you two put together.

Notice how Alison is standing at the ironing board, smoking thoughtfully, waiting for this, which she knows cannot be avoided now Jimmy is launched into his past. Cliff valiantly seeks to turn the issue yet again:

> CLIFF: Who did?

But Alison, aware of its inevitability resignedly gives him his cue:

> ALISON: Madeline.

*See notes and glossary to Act One, p.21.

Jimmy is now launched, and the description which follows is of a figure in his mind. People are transformed by his half-digested education into mythical roles in a personal history idealised in the face of his present sense of meaninglessness.

> JIMMY: Her curiosity about things and about people was staggering. It wasn't just a naïve nosiness. With her, it was simply the delight of being awake and watching.
> [*Alison starts to press Cliff's trousers*]
> CLIFF: [*behind paper*] Perhaps I will make some tea, after all.
> JIMMY: [*quietly*] Just to be with her was an adventure. Even to sit on the top of a bus with her was like setting out with Ulysses.   (p.19)

In this exchange Osborne employs the limitations of the naturalist form to serve his purposes. In a scene like this it would appear as though Jimmy Porter were still the single and sole focus of the action, if we were to judge by the words on the page alone. But through a number of significantly placed pieces of action for Alison and Cliff, and through the implied tone and attitude with which they greet Jimmy's tales from the past, the focus is shifted strongly, so that a resigned yet critical response emerges.

Implicit is their awareness of the way in which Jimmy is idealising what is clearly his own innate curiosity and responsiveness, a curiosity and responsiveness posssessed by all eighteen-years-olds, especially those with the drive and intelligence to secure an affair with a twenty-eight-year-old woman. What is focused here through their response is Jimmy's failure to separate a true understanding of his own past from his continual tendency to idealise and place on pedestals of memory all those figures with which he associates that past. From behind his description of each of them emerges a shadowy second image, a hinted portrait of the real people whom we glimpse through the idealistic memory of Jimmy Porter.

Exactly the same process of idealising and falsifying memory obscures each of the figures to whom Jimmy refers, and through whom he is shown to be bound inescapably to a past from which he cannot free himself: Hugh; Mrs Tanner, Hugh's mother; and above all, his own father. Perhaps the most touching instance of this process is in the account he gives Helena in Act Two Scene One (p.59) of his father's death, significantly focused as a parallel experience by the hints given earlier of the struggle between him and his mother ('My mother was all for being associated with minorities, provided they were the smart, fashionable ones') (p.57). Behind this speech is a hint that his father's attachment to the 'good, brave cause' of the working classes in Spain was a highly selfconscious rejection of a different origin. Note the economic and class implications of the comment (pp.57-8) that 'The family sent him a cheque every month, and hoped he'd get on with it quietly, without too much vulgar fuss.' Through this net of qualifying comments the image of the father he hero-worshipped dissolves into a figure of horror for the small boy, the recipient of a heritage of bitterness and failure which fascinates him and which he tries to understand and idealise in vain:

> 'All that that feverish failure of a man had to listen to him was a small frightened boy. I spent hour upon hour in that tiny bedroom. He would talk to me for hours, pouring out all that was left of his life to one, lonely, bewildered little boy, who could barely understand half of what he said. All he could feel was the despair and the bitterness, the sweet, sickly smell of a dying man . . .' (p.58)

What follows is the moment of acknowledgement of defeat in everything but a mutual destruction. And the appeal he makes now to Alison frankly accepts the false and broken nature of his escape into the past.

> 'Doesn't it matter to you what people do to me? What are you trying to do to me? I've given you just everything. Doesn't it mean *anything* to you?' (p.58)

It is not that the action has drawn us into sympathy with Jimmy, but that it has allowed for the first time the real and genuine nature of the personal dilemma from which his anguish stems to be made clear. So that when Jimmy poses his question, that of how far human sympathy should go, we are at the very least torn with a confusion that seemed, on the surface, to have no part in our response to the Jimmy of Act One, a response incidentally which he articulates like an echo of our own earlier impatience and disgust:

> I rage and shout me head off, and everyone thinks 'poor chap' or 'what an objectionable young man'. But that girl there can twist your arm off with her silence. I've sat in this chair in the dark for hours. And although she knows I'm feeling as I feel now, she's turned over and gone to sleep. [*He gets up and faces Cliff, who doesn't look up from his paper*] One of us is crazy. One of us is mean and stupid and crazy. Which is it? Is it me? Is it me, standing here like an hysterical girl, hardly able to get my words out? Or is it her? Sitting there, putting on her shoes to go out with that . . . [*But inspiration has deserted him now*] Which is it?
> [*Cliff is still looking down at his paper*]
> I wish to heaven you'd try loving her, that's all. (p.59)

The violence of the anger which follows is mitigated by this, the only admission in the play of the love between them both.

The complexity and the subtlety of response which is focused here at the end of Act Two Scene One is the direct result of the careful preparation of the character of Jimmy and the detailed way in which we have been shown his self-destructive and delusory involvement with the past throughout the apparently simple, expository scenes of Act One.

Returning to the opening Act from which this complex network of dramatic effects takes its origin, we may begin to see that Jimmy is trapped between his sense of a past which he idealises, and from which he is, of course, excluded, since it is a falsified one, and the absence in the world in which he has to live of any ideals that can replace his idealised version of that past. The energy which memories alone can release has nowhere to go and turns into a blind fury of provocation, lashing out indiscriminately at anything and everything around him. As the opening act makes clear the destructive impulse is often sought in the smallest event, but it is not necessarily a cold and deliberately calculated act. We are fooled by Jimmy's ability to give expression to passions and feelings which in most of us stay safely and obscurely behind the gate of our teeth, so that we believe that he is in control of the processes which move him. Yet as the play goes on we are forced to see that this control is illusory, and that the real image is that which ends Act Two, when he flings the bear down-stage and it mechanically grinds out an involuntary, stifled groan. This process can be illustrated in the culminating action of the first act.

Jimmy's technique of defensive offence

Having failed to provoke a response to cover the boredom and frustration he feels with his own existence, significantly stressed by the atmosphere of the opening setting in the small, dull, Midland flat, Jimmy turns his attention to one small event after another, seeking any outlet for the obscure sense of purposelessness which drives him. His opening attack on Alison's family (pp.20-1) fails because it is too well known, already absorbed and covered by habit. It begins with a stage direction which sets the scene in detail:

> [*There is no sound, only the plod of Alison's iron. Her eyes are fixed on what she is doing. Cliff stares at the floor. His cheerfulness has deserted him for the moment. Jimmy is rather shakily triumphant. He cannot allow himself to look at either of them to catch their response to his rhetoric, so he moves across to the window, to recover himself, and look out.*]
>
> It's started to rain. That's all it needs. This room and the rain.
>
> [*He's been cheated out of his response, but he's got to draw blood somehow.*]
>
> [*Conversationally*] Yes, that's the little woman's family. You know Mummy and Daddy, of course. And don't let the Marquess of

Queensberry manner fool you. They'll kick you in the groin while you're handing the hat to the maid. As for Nigel and Alison . . . [*in a reverent, Stuart Hibberd voice*] Nigel and Alison. They're what they sound like: sycophantic, phlegmatic and pusillanimous.

CLIFF: I'll bet that concert's started by now. Shall I put it on?

But the subject is too old, and although for one moment it looks as though Jimmy will succeed in getting a response from Alison, she is able to contain and limit it.

Through the section which follows the concert becomes the focus for the attack, with Jimmy switching it on and then using each of their sounds or movements to suggest a personal attack on himself:

JIMMY: Are you going to be much longer with that?
ALISON: Why?
JIMMY: Perhaps you hadn't noticed, but it's interfering with the radio.

With this as a pretext Jimmy launches into his first attack on women:

. . . When you see a woman in front of her bedroom mirror, you realise what a refined sort of a butcher she is [*Turns in*] Did you ever see some dirty old Arab, sticking his fingers into some mess of lamb fat and gristle? Well, she's just like that. Thank God they don't have women surgeons! Those primitive hands would have your guts out in no time. Flip! Out it comes, like the powder out of its box. Flop! Back it goes, like the powder puff on the table.

CLIFF: [*grimacing cheerfully*] Ugh! Stop it!
JIMMY: [*moving upstage*] She'd drop your guts like hair clips and fluff all over the floor. You've got to be fundamentally insensitive to be as noisy and as clumsy as that.

It is to this primitiveness in woman that Jimmy's attacks are directed. In his later image of Alison as a python, a reptilian snake swallowing him alive when he makes love to her (p.37), there is the same basic response. Buried here is not only a clue to a psychological fear that Jimmy clearly brings to sexual relationships, a fear made clear as part of his sense of betrayal in his comments on his mother's attitude to his father in Act 2 Scene 1 (p.57), but one which is modified through the Shavian parallel, implicitly drawn between Jimmy's attitude and that of Tanner in *Man and Superman*. Jimmy, at one level, clearly sees himself as the Superman writ small, and sees the struggle between man and woman at least implicitly as the struggle between creative sensitivity and the blind instinctive forces which swallow up the future in a stifling obsession with the biological urges of the present. Osborne, as others have commented, is more indebted to Shaw than often appears. The intellectual patterns, though, remain at the level of obscure allusion, and it would be difficult to see this as more than an echo which colours but does not construct the effects that it serves. Perhaps Katherine J. Worth's comment best sums up the nature of this debt when she refers to a quality in the speeches of Jimmy Porter which seems to owe such a debt. She comments: 'Jimmy Porter's long speeches are at the same time violent and controlled, sardonically humorous and in deadly earnest, evoking occasional echoes of both Shaw and Strindberg.'*

Jimmy's tirade against the female culminates in his image of the girls who once had a flat above him, and who drove him mad with their slamming and stamping, 'the eternal bloody racket of the female'. Right on cue the church bells begin their clanging. Jimmy instantly switches his attack, but the language subtly employs the bells as a symbolic representation of the 'female racket'. Through the figure of the vigilant, life-hating landlady Mrs Drury (are we to understand that there is a buried image of the respectable old theatre here?)† Osborne draws an allusion between the female demand for an instant and regulated acknowledgement of the demands of the present and the respectable clamour which the church bells have substituted for the pure noise that people make when they are truly themselves, and which is clearly here (as in the later play *The Entertainer*) associated with the sound of jazz, represented in the play by Jimmy's trumpet-playing.

JIMMY: Oh, hell! Now the bloody bells have started!
[*He rushes to the window*]
Wrap it up, will you? Stop ringing those bells! There's somebody going crazy in here! I don't want to hear them!
ALISON: Stop shouting! [*Recovering immediately*] You'll have Mrs Drury up here.
JIMMY: I don't give a damn about Mrs Drury—that mild old gentlewoman doesn't fool me, even if she takes in you two. She's an old robber. She gets more than enough out of us for this place every week. Anyway, she's probably in church [*points to the window*] swinging on those bloody bells! (p.25)

The relationship between Cliff and Alison

The action that erupts at the end of Act I is the first clear indication of the tenderness in Jimmy which has been buried so far beneath the free-booting cruelty and cheerful malice of the earlier action. The routine of Alison's ironing is broken just as the routine of Jimmy's attack on those close to him is broken by Cliff's attempt to drive Jimmy from the cover of his despair through humour.

*Katherine J. Worth, 'The Angry Young Man', in *Look Back in Anger* (Macmillan Casebook Series), ed. J. Russell Taylor, Macmillan, London, 1968.
†See comment on 'Miss Drury', p.22.

CLIFF: Well, shall we dance? [*He pushes Jimmy round the floor, who is past the mood for this kind of fooling*] Do you come here often?
JIMMY: Only in the mating season. All right, all right, very funny [*He tries to escape but Cliff holds him like a vice*] Let me go.
CLIFF: Not until you've apologised for being nasty to everyone. Do you think bosoms will be in or out, this year?
JIMMY: Your teeth will be out in a minute, if you don't let go!
(pp.25–6)

The sudden reversal of feeling which follows Alison's being hurt in the struggle between the two men is one of the most violent shifts in language in the play. The fact that Osborne employs what on the surface is an apparent cliché is less important than the fact that Jimmy, who uses it, talks usually neither in terms of endearment nor in clichés.

CLIFF: [*picking himself up*] She's hurt. Are you all right?
ALISON: Well, does it look like it!
CLIFF: She's burnt her arm on the iron.
JIMMY: Darling, I'm sorry.
ALISON: Get out!
JIMMY: I'm sorry, believe me. You think I did it on purpose.
ALISON: [*her head shaking helplessly*] Clear out of my SIGHT!
[*He stares at her uncertainly. Cliff nods to him, and he turns and goes out of the door*] (p.26)

This is the scene too in which we are shown more of both Alison and Cliff than we have seen in the play so far. Again, this process employs reaction rather than direct revelation of character. It is in reaction to Jimmy's statements that the characters are exposed.

CLIFF: Here we are then. Let's have your arm.
[*He kneels down beside her, and she holds out her arm*]
I've put it under the tap. It's quite soft. I'll do it ever so gently.
[*Very carefully, he rubs the soap over the burn*] All right? [*She nods*]
You're a brave girl.
ALISON: I don't feel very brave. [*tears harshening her voice*] I really don't Cliff. I don't think I can take much more. [*Turns her head away*] I think I feel rather sick.
CLIFF: All over now. [*Puts the soap down*] Would you like me to get you something?
[*She shakes her head. He sits on the arm of the chair, and puts his arm around her. She leans her head back on to him*]
Don't upset yourself, lovely.
[*He massages the back of her neck, and she lets her head fall forward*]
(p.27)

In a small section like this we see how both Cliff's and Alison's dependence on one another is strengthened by the roles they are able to adopt. Alison here slips very easily back into the role of the small girl and Cliff assumes the role of the father, yet this too is as much play-acting as the bears and squirrels which are later to be shown to be the substitute for the real 'human enthusiasm' that Jimmy has demanded from all of them.

The failure of the roles to sustain the characters is shown in the fact that Alison and Cliff immediately reverse their positions. She leans back and closes her eyes again.

ALISON: Bless you. [*He kisses the top of her head*]

Cliff reveals his own very strong dependence on both Alison and Jimmy in the speech which follows:

CLIFF: I don't think I'd have the courage to live on my own again in spite of everything. I'm pretty rough, and pretty ordinary really, and I'd seem worse on my own. And you get fond of people too, worse luck.

It is this final comment that Alison picks up when she replies, 'I don't think I want anything more to do with love any more. I can't take it on.' Cliff reverts to the father role in the following speech:

CLIFF: You're too young to start giving up. Too young, and too lovely. Perhaps I'd better put a bandage on that, do you think so? (pp.27–8)

But there has been there, at that point in the play, a moment that is never to recur when Cliff comes close to revealing a sexual love for Alison but it is a moment that fades with Alison's denial of that possibility and is not referred to again until Alison's lengthy explanation to Helena in Act Two Scene One of the relationship between Cliff and herself:

ALISON: He had his own jazz band once. That was when he was still a student, before I knew him. I rather think he'd like to start another, and give up the stall altogether.
HELENA: Is Cliff in love with you?
ALISON: [*Stops brushing for a moment*] No . . . I don't think so.
HELENA: And what about you? You look as though I've asked you a rather peculiar question. The way things are, you might as well be frank with me. I only want to help. After all, your behaviour together is a little strange by most people's standards, to say the least.
ALISON: You mean you've seen us embracing each other?
HELENA: Well, it doesn't seem to go on as much as it did, I admit. Perhaps he finds my presence inhibiting even if Jimmy's isn't.
ALISON: We're simply fond of each other, there's no more to it than that.

HELENA: Darling, really! It can't be as simple as that.
ALISON: You mean there must be something physical too? I suppose there is, but it's not exactly a consuming passion with either of us. It's just a relaxed, cheerful sort of thing, like being warm in bed. You're too comfortable to bother about moving for the sake of some other pleasure.
HELENA: I find it difficult to believe anyone's that lazy!
ALISON: I think *we* are.   (pp.41–2)

Finally, what Alison is seeking to express to Helena at that moment, is that there is not a physical or indeed even a sexual passion between Cliff and herself but that they are fundamentally more concerned with the peace that they can attain by restraint rather than the pleasure they might enjoy through fulfilment. In a real way they are proving in their relationship the truth of Jimmy's assertion that 'Nobody can be bothered. No one can raise themselves out of their delicious sloth'. Significantly, that quotation is followed by a direct attack on Alison and Cliff:

JIMMY: You two will drive me round the bend soon . . . I know it, as sure as I'm sitting here. I know you're going to drive me mad. (p.15)

And the action of the play underlines the fact that the burn which has been received by Alison at the end of Act One is as least as much the fault of Cliff as the fault of Jimmy. This is not to assert that Cliff and Alison are attacked as characters at this point in the play but rather that they are shown to be as complex in their own way and in their reactions to Jimmy as he himself is and as much involved in the creation of the situation that they must all endure. It is, of course, here at the end of Act One that Alison reveals for the first time to Cliff that she has realised that she is pregnant. Cliff acts out the role that is normally assigned to the lover in such situations.

CLIFF: What are you going to do?
ALISON: I've no idea.
CLIFF: [*Having cut her bandage, he starts tying it*] That too tight?
ALISON: Fine, thank you. [*She rises, goes to the ironing board, folds it up, and leans it against the food cupboard*]
CLIFF: Is it . . . Is it . . .?
ALISON: Too late to avert the situation? [*Places the iron on the rack of the stove*] I'm not certain yet. Maybe not. If not, there won't be any problems, will there?
CLIFF: And if it is too late?
[*Her face is turned away from him. She simply shakes her head*] (p.29)

In a peculiar way, Cliff, at this point in the play, has become a means of showing that tenderness and love for Alison which Jimmy so clearly possesses and is yet unable to express to her in a direct way. When Jimmy returns we are shown the only form in which he and Alison can express the love they have for one another. Jimmy is beginning, almost automatically, to move back towards the aggressive mood which has dominated the action of the play to this point and which has only been broken by the accident with the ironing board. It is in reaction to Alison's alarm at this new aggression that Jimmy's tenderness is revealed.

The fantasy world of Jimmy and Alison

JIMMY: . . . and there's Hugh's mum, of course. I'd almost forgotten her. She's been a good friend to us, if you like. She's even letting me buy the sweet-stall off her in my own time. She only bought it for us, anyway. She's so fond of you. I can never understand why you're so —distant with her.

ALISON: [*alarmed at this threat of a different mood*] Jimmy—please no!

JIMMY: [*staring at her anxious face*] You're very beautiful. A beautiful, great-eyed squirrel. [*She nods brightly, relieved*] Hoarding, nut-munching squirrel. [*She mimes this delightedly*] With polished, gleaming fur, and an ostrich feather of a tail.

ALISON: Wheeeeeeee!

JIMMY: How I envy you. [*He stands, her arms around his neck*]

ALISON: Well, you're a jolly super bear, too. A really sooooooooooooooooper, marvellous bear.

JIMMY: Bears and squirrels ARE marvellous.

ALISON: Marvellous AND beautiful.   (pp.33-4)

This world of squirrels and bears has been the only refuge to which they have always been able to retreat. These scenes are difficult to reconcile at first with the angry, swinging cruelty of the opening of Act One and yet the psychology is clearly delineated. The childish, insistent demands of Jimmy, the need to eat for comfort, to which Cliff draws attention, the strongly asserted dependence on characters from the past, all point in the same direction, and it is a direction which naturally leads to this defensive world of imaginary furry little animals. The make-believe game of bears and squirrels is more than a retreat from an intolerable situation in their marriage. It is an expression of a mutual dependence, a dependence which stems in Jimmy's case from his failure to relate to his father. In Alison's case, although the action buries the implication deeper than in Jimmy's, a similar point is underlined. In Act Two Scene Two, for example, when Alison's father has arrived to take her home, a clear indication of the identical roles they have played in their respective marriages is brought out:

COLONEL: . . . Perhaps you and I were the ones most to blame.
ALISON: You and I!
COLONEL: I think you may take after me a little my dear. You like to sit on the fence because it's comfortable and more peaceful.
ALISON: Sitting on the fence! I married him, didn't I?
COLONEL: Oh yes, you did.   (p.66)

Once again, the action of the play points to a complex situation in which Jimmy's reaction and Jimmy's character is only one factor. By the end of Act One, we have learned that Cliff and Alison are not merely ciphers.

Helena, and what she reveals about Jimmy's attitude to women

The arrival of Helena at the end of the act is of course necessary to pick up the underlying continuing struggle, the revelation of which is the main point of the whole exposition. Jimmy introduces the violent attack on Alison, with which the act ends, in a rather peculiar way. In a speech which contains more intellectual references and allusions than any other in the play so far, he launches into yet another of his violent attacks on 'women':

JIMMY: What does she want? What would make her ring up? It can't be for anything pleasant. Oh well, we shall soon know. [*He settles on the table*] Few minutes ago things didn't seem so bad either. I've just about had enough of this 'expense of spirit' lark, as far as women are concerned. Honestly, it's enough to make you become a scoutmaster or something isn't it? Sometimes I almost envy old Gide and the Greek Chorus boys. Oh, I'm not saying that it mustn't be hell for them a lot of the time. But, at least they do seem to have a cause—not a particularly good one, it's true. But plenty of them do seem to have a revolutionary fire about them, which is more than you can say for the rest of us. Like Webster, for instance. He doesn't like me—they hardly ever do.
[*He is talking for the sake of it, only half listening to what he is saying*] I dare say he suspects me because I refuse to treat him either as a clown or as a tragic hero. He's like a man with a strawberry mark—he keeps thrusting it in your face because he can't believe it doesn't interest or horrify you particularly. [*Picks up Alison's handbag thoughtfully, and starts looking through it*] As if I give a damn which way he likes his meat served up. I've got my own strawberry mark—only it's in a different place. No, as far as the Michelangelo Brigade's concerned, I must be a sort of right-wing deviationist. If the Revolution ever comes, I'll be the first to be put up against the wall, with all the other poor old liberals.   (pp.35–6)

Like the other attacks on women in the play, these remarks are not so much a means of describing Jimmy's real feeling about the opposite sex as a means of revealing his own refusal to allow Alison or anyone else to discover his need for them. Here the buried references to Jimmy's mother in Act Two Scene One are obviously important.

> JIMMY: . . . as for my mother, all she could think about was the fact that she had allied herself to a man who seemed to be on the wrong side in all things. My mother was all for being associated with minorities, provided they were the smart, fashionable ones.   (p.57)

The image of the mother presented here is clearly one which involves Jimmy in a notion of betrayal. The father has been betrayed by the mother and he fears that the same process of betrayal must occur as an inevitable part of all relationships. In this sense, as well as in a social and political sense, he looks back in anger to the past and it is this which effectually bars him from any possibility of a future. Unless we realise this level in the action, we are not able to understand the vehemence of Jimmy's anger at the end of Act One. After all, on the surface of the play what provokes the violent attack is simply the arrival of one of his wife's friends, but beneath this there is the basic fear of any figure from the past who has not been tested for loyalties. It is Jimmy's need to test the past and the figures who inhabit it before they are permitted to become part of his private mythology that is referred to by Alison in Act Two Scene One:

> HELENA: And what about Jimmy? After all, he is your husband. Do you mean to say he actually approves of it?
> ALISON: It isn't easy to explain. It's what he would call a question of allegiances, and he expects you to be pretty literal about them. Not only about himself and all the things he believes in, his present and his future, but his past as well. All the people he admires and loves, and has loved. The friends he used to know, people I've never even known—and probably wouldn't have liked. His father, who died years ago. Even the other women he's loved.   (p.42)

The dramatic irony of the final speech, in which Jimmy prays that Alison may conceive a child that will die, is an appalling image for an audience to absorb.

> JIMMY: . . . If you could have a child, and it would die. Let it grow, let a recognisable human face emerge from that little mass of india-rubber and wrinkles. [*She retreats away from him*] Please—if only I could watch you face that. I wonder if you might even become a recognisable human being yourself. But I doubt it. [*She moves away, stunned, and leans on the gas stove down L. He stands rather helplessly on his own*] (p.37)

The second part of the final speech of Act One is in a subtly different mood. Jimmy, standing on his own, is helpless, and this fact dominates the tone of the following speech. He is making a cry for help rather than continuing the attack of the earlier part of the speech, and the momentum which it gathers makes the end of the speech a violent and angry outburst which is the greatest example of the process of Jimmy's whole character, from helplessness through anger into cruelty.

> JIMMY: Do you know I have never known the great pleasure of love-making when I didn't desire it myself. Oh, it's not that she hasn't her own kind of passion. She has the passion of a python. She just devours me whole every time, as if I were some over-large rabbit. That's me. That bulge around her navel—if you're wondering what it is—it's me. Me, buried alive down there, and going mad, smothered in that peaceful looking coil. Not a sound, not a flicker from her—she doesn't even rumble a little. You'd think that this indigestible mess would stir up some kind of tremor in those distended, overfed tripes—but not her! [*Crosses up to the door*] She'll go on sleeping and devouring until there's nothing left of me. (pp.37–8)

By the end of Act One the author has provided the actor with all the opportunities he needs to bring out the complicated characterisation required by the opening stage direction and part of this process has been the use of Cliff and Alison to mark and comment on the action.

Jimmy Porter as a representative figure

Because Jimmy's character is so complex, it is insufficient to dismiss him, as many critics have, as merely 'a spokesman for his generation'. There is certainly a strong connection between the individual and psychological problems he faces, and the problems of a whole genera-tion of people in the early 1950s. The spread of educational opportuni-ties, which on the surface might have been seen as only desirable, had an unfortunate side-effect. Jimmy is an example of those people who, born into the working class, were educated out of it, but were unable to find an acceptable role in the complexities of the English class system. In the flawed world of post-war England, these people had no place to go. As a result, Jimmy Porter sentimentalises the working class because he is no longer part of it. The sweet stall at which he works is a means of making concrete this romantic quality in Jimmy's response to the work-ing class. Cliff, who is genuinely working class and has remained so, knows how inadequate the gesture is—playing at being proletarian by a man who has been dispossessed by his education: 'The sweet stall's all right but I think I'd like to try something else. You're highly edu-cated and it suits you. But I need something a bit better' (p.83). Jimmy belongs to no world. There is no route back for him into the working-class world of his childhood, and he thinks even this is suspect since his father and mother are clearly working-class élite. The alternative, the world of the middle/upper classes, is also impossible; that world can provide no refuge for him either. It can produce enemies, and so a struggle, but he cannot belong here, since to do so he would have to betray his past. To love Alison and her mother, he would have to reject his father and Mrs Tanner, and he can do neither. He is trapped in the limbo of no class and no loyalty. Hence his tendency, which Alison notices and comments on to Helena, to create a personal myth about those people to whom he can be loyal. Jimmy retreats to his myth when, for example, he is betrayed into revealing his love for Alison at the end of Act One:

> JIMMY: He's the only friend I seem to have left now. People go away. You never see them again. I can remember lots of names—men and women. When I was at school—Watson, Roberts, Davies, Jenny, Madeline, Hugh [*pause*] and there's Hugh's mum, of course, I'd almost forgotten her. (pp.33–4)

But this retreat is a dangerous one since it leads him into a recognition that those friends are members of the opposite camp from that to which Alison belongs, and hence the shift to the attack:

> JIMMY: . . . She's so fond of you. I can never understand why you're so—distant with her.

When Alison responds with alarm at this potential attack, Jimmy, equally anxious to avoid conflict and genuinely wishing to be able to show his love for Alison, shifts to the only world that they can inhabit simultaneously, the fantasy world, the womb-like, comfortable world of squirrels and bears. The attempt to forge a link between the two worlds, which Jimmy's speech reveals, is doomed to failure and here, at the end of Act One, we are already clearly aware that the only possible solution is a retreat into fantasy, the same retreat which concludes the action of the play. Jimmy's anger in Act One is the product of desperation and its horror lies in the fact that he knows, as Alison does, that he is engaged in destroying both of them, himself as much as her. The only refuge is a return to the womb of fantasy, and the image of Alison's passion devouring him wholly expresses his own disgust at his inability to go anywhere else. Her love, in all its sincerity and force, devours him and he hates her for it, although he knows it is not her fault. Although much of the explanation of the condition between the couple is held over to Act Two, here, at the end of Act One, we have been given all the information we need to understand the relationship between Alison and Jimmy, in all its personal and social complexity.

The naturalist structure of *Look Back in Anger*

Naturalist plays suffer from a disadvantage because of their need to maintain a credible illusion of reality. In a play which does not claim to be an imitation of real life, information can be communicated to an audience directly and simply through some formal, conventional technique, for example the soliloquy, in which a character can speak his or her thoughts aloud; or the 'conversation' between two characters whose function is solely to impart necessary information, as with the two gentlemen at the beginning of Shakespeare's *Cymbeline*; the aside, too, can be employed to convey information or comment. Much of the information so communicated may concern events or people who are not part of the action being presented on stage, but who form significant parts of the past lives of the characters the play explores. In a naturalist play, such as *Look Back in Anger*, other techniques are required.

Much of the information the play provides about the past relationship of Jimmy and Alison is held over until Act Two. Helena's first function in the play is to be the recipient of the information Osborne wishes to convey to the audience about Jimmy and Alison. Obviously, to preserve the naturalist illusion it would be impossible for Cliff to serve this function. As an old friend and one who has been living with them for a considerable period of time he would be likely to have learned all about the past already. With Helena's entrance it is possible for Osborne to introduce this past material in a credible dialogue, first, between Alison and Helena and, later, between Helena and Jimmy. The information Alison provides about her first encounters with Jimmy helps to enrich our understanding of him, though it is hard at first to reconcile the image she creates with the defeated, brawling animal of Act One.

Alison's past relationship with Jimmy

When Helena asks Alison why she married him, she gives a description of Jimmy which recaptures the fascination, and the complexity of her original response to him.

> I met him at a party. I remember it so clearly. I was almost twenty-one. The men there all looked as if they distrusted him, and as for the women, they were all intent on showing their contempt for this rather odd creature, but no one seemed quite sure how to do it. He'd come to the party on a bicycle, he told me, and there was oil all over his dinner jacket. It had been such a lovely day, and he'd been in the sun. Everything about him seemed to burn, his face, the edges of his hair glistened and seemed to spring off his head, and his eyes were so blue and full of the sun. He looked so young and frail, in spite of the

tired line of his mouth. I knew I was taking on more than I was ever likely to be capable of bearing, but there never seemed to be any choice. (p.45)

The language which Alison uses when she talks of Jimmy illustrates very clearly her confused response to the situation she finds herself in. The imagery of barbarian hordes, raiding the polite parties, 'plundering them, wolfing their food and drinks, and smoking their cigars like ruffians' (p.44), modulates into a vision of Jimmy as a knight in armour 'with his axe swinging round his head—frail and so full of fire'. It was 'The old story of the knight in shining armour—except that his armour didn't really shine very much' (p.45). Alison is aware that her fascination is potentially self-destructive from the start, and she is aware of the impossibility of reconciling her real perception of Jimmy with the dream image she retains. Alison understands quite clearly at one level that Jimmy cannot really ever become part of her world, nor even really accept her, without betraying the past to which he looks back in frustrated anger. She is able to explain to Helena much of the inside workings of Jimmy. The audience is drawn into a sense of how much Alison really does understand of the impossibility of her situation, and the sources for this in Jimmy's personality. At this point in time Alison shows a depth of understanding that Helena will never be able to achieve.

HELENA: And what about Jimmy? After all, he is your husband. Do you mean to say he actually approves of it?
ALISON: It isn't easy to explain. It's what he would call a question of allegiances, and he expects you to be pretty literal about them. Not only about himself and all the things he believes in, his present and his future, but his past as well. All the people he admires and loves, and has loved. The friends he used to know, people I've never even known —and probably wouldn't have liked. His father, who died years ago. Even the other women he's loved. (p.42)

Alison's awareness of the problems in their relationship

A speech of this nature provides the audience with very deep insights into Jimmy's condition. We learn more about Jimmy from Alison in this scene than we have learnt so far in the play. And in so doing we also learn how deep the relationship between them really is. She even shows that she is aware of why they have to retreat into the fantasy world of bears and squirrels, and why this retreat too is doomed.

ALISON: [pointing to the chest of drawers up R] You see that bear, and that squirrel? Well, that's him, and that's me.
HELENA: Meaning?

ALISON: The game we play: bears and squirrels, squirrels and bears.
[*Helena looks rather blank*]
Yes, it's quite mad, I know. Quite mad. [*Picks up the two animals*]
That's him ... And that's me ...
HELENA: I didn't realise he was a bit fey, as well as everything else!
ALISON: Oh, there's nothing fey about Jimmy. It's just all we seem to
have left. Or had left. Even bears and squirrels seem to have gone
their own ways now. (p.47)

Alison shows that she is well aware of the escapist nature of the fantasy,
and the way in which it serves to allow them to express a love for each
other which they cannot express when their social, intellectual and
personal differences are visible to each other. As she says:

... We could become little furry creatures with little furry brains.
Full of dumb, uncomplicated affection for each other. Playful, care-
less creatures in their own cosy zoo for two. A silly symphony for
people who couldn't bear the pain of being human beings any longer.
And now, even they are dead, poor little silly animals. They were all
love and no brains. [*Puts them back*]   (p.47)

Even here Alison shows that she is aware that no woman can ever really
satisfy Jimmy, since, as the fantasy illustrates, he is searching for a
womb-like retreat, and yet is driven to anger by the woman who offers
it him. All Alison, or any woman, can offer Jimmy is sexual love and an
image of comfort, and he will hate her for 'smothering' him even while
he self-destructively demands the 'security' of her love. This moment
in the play foreshadows the more complete realisation, when Alison
talks with Helena at the end of Act Three. As she realises then, Jimmy
needs some impossible amalgam of mother, lover and intellectual
companion, or, as Alison puts it, 'a kind of cross between a mother and
a Greek courtesan, a henchwoman, a mixture of Cleopatra and
Boswell' (p.91).

Jimmy's social alienation

Jimmy's education has forced him out of one world, and yet simultaneously barred him from accepting the alternative world of Alison's
mother and her brother Nigel, 'the Platitude from Outer Space' and
Conservative Member of Parliament. Jimmy Porter has the quintes-
sential modern mind, sharp and sentimental, witty and maudlin by turns,
a wheel spinning fruitlessly in the mud, flinging it purposelessly in the
face of anyone who comes near and then crying out in terror at the
thought of being left alone in the dark. Characteristically Jimmy hates
both the society people, Mummy, brother Nigel ... and the 'intel-
lectuals', whom he identifies with the 'posh' Sunday papers. The former

betray his educated loyalty to the truth and to ideas, but the latter betray his sentimental longing for a lost world of ideals and emotional unity in a cause which he identifies as 'working-class' unity. Helena performs an important function here in that she combines both stances in one figure. She is modern, intellectual to some degree, but not dispossessed of her identity. She stands in a secure place, symbolised by her un-questioning acceptance of the moral categories of religion, even when she does not *act* on them. Yet her strength lies in her essential hypocrisy. Jimmy's attack on her sentimental Christianity is also very *self*-reveal-ing, since the things of which he accuses Helena are very close to his own habit of idealising the past.

> You see, I know Helena and her kind so very well. In fact, her kind are everywhere, you can't move for them. They're a romantic lot. They spend their time mostly looking forward to the past. The only place they can see the light is the Dark Ages. She's moved long ago into a lovely little cottage of the soul, cut right off from the ugly problems of the twentieth century altogether. She prefers to be cut off from all the conveniences we've fought to get for centuries. She'd rather go down to the ecstatic little shed at the bottom of the garden to relieve her sense of guilt. Our Helena is full of ecstatic wind . . .
>
> (p.56)

Even if Jimmy fails to see the closeness of this attack to his own flaws the audience does not. In his own way, we are reminded, Jimmy is as much of a sentimental snob as Helena, even if his snobbery is inverted.

The sentimental idealism of Jimmy

Jimmy's account of his father's death which follows is moving and and revelatory but it is not offered by Osborne as a full explanation of Jimmy's position. We are not meant to take Jimmy's statements at their simple face value. By this time in the play the complex interaction of character and event has provided us with a means of viewing Jimmy's rhetoric through alternative eyes. Despite his assertions we are well aware by this time that what excluded Jimmy Porter is not Helena, nor Alison, nor even their mothers and fathers, but rather his *own* dis-illusionment with the causes for which *his* father bled. He looks back in anger because he cannot find his way back, except by a process of sentimental idealising, to a world where beliefs can be simply accepted and acted upon. He is crucified on the pin of his own intellect. All the complicated information he gleans from the 'posh' Sundays serves only to make the possibility of any significant choice of action recede farther and farther away. What Jimmy Porter longs to do is to be able to see less clearly so that he could content himself with the half-truths of either his father's world, or that of brother Nigel, but he cannot rest easy with either. His awareness and sensitivity serve only to expose in acts of senseless cruelty the weaknesses and inadequacy of those around him. When he has finally destroyed all the possible shelters, there will be nothing left to destroy but himself.

> . . . One of us is crazy. One of us is mean and stupid and crazy. Which is it? Is it me? Is it me, standing here like an hysterical girl, hardly able to get my words out? Or is it her? Sitting there, putting on her shoes to go out with that . . . [*But inspiration has deserted him now*] Which is it?
> [*Cliff is still looking down at his paper*]
> I wish to heaven you'd try loving her that's all.   (p.59)

At moments like this there can be little doubt of the genuine nature of the anguish and torment which Jimmy Porter feels.

Jimmy's attack on Alison, and his relationship with Helena

Jimmy's outburst against Alison which follows, his desire to be able to 'stand up in your tears, and splash about in them, and sing' is a demand that she strip away the last of her defences and join him wholly in his agony and despair. He wants Alison to give away her refuges too —her silence, her ability to *accept* life, her links with her secure past. Yet even when he makes this demand he is aware that there is nowhere this can lead except to their mutual destruction. Alison acknowledges this in her images of Jimmy as raider and barbarian. The point is reinforced at the end of Act Two when she seeks to explain to her father the nature of the attraction between Jimmy and herself.

> . . . for twenty years, I'd lived a happy, uncomplicated life, and suddenly, this—this spiritual barbarian—throws down the gauntlet at me. Perhaps only another woman could understand what a challenge like that means—although I think Helena was as mystified as you are.   (p.67)

Her father, aware that Alison is no longer the 'happy, uncomplicated' person whose loss she regrets, and aware, too, that she will not be able to discard the relationship with Jimmy as easily as she may suppose, tries, gently, to warn her of the need to be sure of her decision.

> This is a big step you're taking. You've made up your mind to come back with me? Is that really what you want?   (p.68)

Helena's entry seems to resolve the situation, and Alison, her decision made, leaves with Colonel Redfern .

Helena is now left alone and is ready to be dispossessed of her assurance. But with Helena the process is always only partial, a ritual which does not touch her deeply. The sudden, passionate outburst of feeling with which the act ends shows how Jimmy's anguish erodes secure, unquestioned values, and illustrates how *even* Helena must pick up the gauntlet of the challenge he embodies, though of course on her own terms.

Helena is the self-destruction Jimmy seeks writ large, as he knows only too well, and as he acknowledges to Cliff in the next act.

> It's a funny thing. You've been loyal, generous and a good friend. But I'm quite prepared to see you wander off, find a new home, and make out on your own. And all because of something I want from that girl downstairs, something I know in my heart she's incapable of giving. You're worth a half a dozen Helenas to me or to anyone. And if you were in my place you'd do the same thing. Right?
> CLIFF: Right.
> JIMMY: Why, why, why do we let these women bleed us to death?
> (p.84)

There is no tenderness in their relationship, not even the possible false escape of squirrels and bears. Their passion is only an aspect of their enmity, a mutually inescapable challenge. And before long they openly acknowledge this.

> You made a good enemy, didn't you? What they call a worthy opponent . . . You stood up and came out to meet me. Oh, Helena— [*His face comes up to hers, and they embrace fiercely*]   (p.86)

But Helena is locked out of the process of mutual self-destruction which is the only real route open to Jimmy. She has enough of the old armour-plating of assurance securely in place to be able to resist Jimmy's demands for final despair. Finally, she is content to retreat to the world of half-truths, where she can live as half a person. When Alison returns, broken and defeated, Helena is confronted with an image of what she would have to become to survive unburned. She does so again, now, yielding place to Alison. She tells her:

> When I saw you standing there tonight, I knew that it was all utterly wrong. That I didn't believe in any of this, and not Jimmy or anyone could make me believe otherwise. [*Rising*] How could I have ever thought I could get away with it! He wants one world and I want another, and lying in that bed won't ever change that.   (p.90)

Helena is a realist, and as such can live with the eroded values of the post-war world, while Jimmy, like Colonel Redfern, is still looking back in anger to the time when idealism and moral passion were capable of shaping a whole life and a whole generation. Helena, who is not stupid, but whose vision is very narrow, gets half the truth when she tells Alison that:

> There's no place for people like that any longer—in sex or politics or anything. That's why he's so futile. Sometimes, when I listen to him, I feel he thinks he's still in the middle of the French Revolution. And that's where he ought to be, of course. He doesn't know where he is or where he's going. He'll never do anything, and he'll never amount to anything. (p.90)

Alison's reply is very sardonic, but it reveals the depths of her understanding of Jimmy in comparison with Helena's. 'I suppose,' she answers, 'he's what you'd call an Eminent Victorian. Slightly comic in a way . . . We seem to have had this conversation before.' Alison's reply draws attention to the fact that it is the moral passion, the demand for a belief that one can wholeheartedly adopt that is the root of Jimmy's despair. What he is searching for is not a role, not a position in life, but a belief, a compelling and complete conviction quite inseparable from his being. It is his tragedy—and the tragedy of the times which the play explores—that such beliefs are no longer possible.

Helena's decision to retreat from the world of pain and suffering which Jimmy offers is therefore in some ways an escape as great as that which Alison and Jimmy engage in when they retreat to the world of squirrels and bears. Jimmy's condemnation of her action (pp.93–4) is a very compelling one.

> JIMMY: [*in a low, resigned voice*] They all want to escape from the pain of being alive. And most of all, from love. [*Crosses to the dressing table*] I always knew something like this would turn up—some problem, like an ill wife—and it would be too much for those delicate hot-house feelings of yours. [*He sweeps up Helena's things from the dressing table, and crosses over to the wardrobe. Outside, the church bells start ringing*] It's no good trying to fool yourself about love. You can't fall into it like a soft job, without dirtying up your hands. [*Hands her the make-up things, which she takes. He opens the wardrobe*] It takes muscle and guts. And if you can't bear the thought [*takes out a dress on a hanger*] of messing up your nice, clean soul, [*crossing back to her*] you'd better give up the whole idea of life, and become a saint. [*Puts the dress in her arms*] Because you'll never make it as a human being. It's either this world or the next. (p.94)

Helena's choice, when she leaves, is reinforced as a false one by the sound of the bells which ring throughout the quiet, low speech. She is going back to an assurance which is false, leaning on institutions and patterns which are already outdated and inadequate.

The difficulties of a solution

But, finally, what alternatives are there? *Look Back In Anger* is not a play putting forward a thesis, and Osborne proffers no solutions for the situation he has recorded. At the end of the play Jimmy is left in despair, needing Alison's love but unable to accept it. In his anguish he cries out to her. 'I may be a lost cause, but I thought if you loved me, it needn't matter' (p.95). Alison is finally able to accept his terms. But those terms, as we have seen, can only lead to a further round of cruelties and erosions which must end in their both being destroyed. Alison's decision to rejoin him in the pit, though on equal terms now, ugly, ridiculous and lost as she feels herself to be, can buy them only a temporary respite. The moment of triumph he has waited for turns to ashes in his mouth, and when she cries out in her despair, the love he cannot deny but finds it impossible to express renders him, literally, speechless:

JIMMY: Don't. Please don't . . . I can't—
[*She gasps for her breath against him*]
You're all right. You're all right now. Please, I—I . . .. Not any more.

(p.96)

The only speech left is the retreat to the resting place, to the world of squirrels and bears, a world that Jimmy knows will be invaded in its turn, a world where there are 'cruel steel traps lying about everywhere, just waiting for rather mad, slightly satanic and very timid little animals' (p.96). This final image reinforces our sense that they both know that there is no escape in this retreat. The ending of the play, then, is not a whimsical tag, but a serious way of stating what the whole pattern of the play has made clear. For Jimmy and Alison the process of destruction is inevitable, for it is a process whose root is in the malaise of the time. 'Poor squirrels', says Jimmy . . . 'Oh poor, poor bears,' replies Alison. Poor confused, cruel, unlovely, self-destructive modern squirrels and bears. Poor you, poor me!

Part 4

Hints for study

The general approach to play reading

Unspoken words

Reading and understanding a play is different from reading other forms of literature. Unlike a novel or a poem the text of a play is not the finished work of art. The play only becomes completed as a finished work of art when it is performed. Thus, the text of a play must be read with a lively awareness of what is implied in the language for realisation on a stage. This process we may call visualising the text of the play. The playwright provides us with a number of very explicit clues to help us in this process. These clues include the description of the stage setting, the stage directions, which may include a wide range of effects from directions to the actor to speak a line with a certain tone, or gesture, to a specific move on stage; finally, the dialogue itself may contain implicit directions to which the reader must also be responsive. For example, Colonel Redfern's speech in which he regrets the passing of his days in India (pp.67–8) contains an implicit direction to the reader to cease focusing his attention on Alison and to go inside himself as he recalls the past. This then allows Alison to refocus his attention with her comment at the end of the speech: 'You're hurt because everything is changed . . .'.

When approaching a play it is necessary to understand the convention of stage presentation within which it operates. In the case of *Look Back in Anger* the convention employed is called the 'naturalist' convention. This means that the audience is asked to accept that what occurs on the stage is a credible imitation of real or natural behaviour. This convention restricts the effects available to the playwright. It lays special emphasis on stage setting to create atmosphere, and on the use of objects on stage to serve as tools for the actor to convey inner emotion which cannot be credibly rendered in speech. Thus, for example, the letter which Alison leaves for Jimmy in Act Two Scene Two (p.70) allows her to make visible the difficulty she has in leaving Jimmy, and her inability to cope with the attack which she knows her action will produce. In a naturalist play, too, it is difficult for the playwright to make large, discursive comments about events which do not immediately affect the action on the stage. The need to maintain a relatively natural level of language restricts the metaphorical density of the language. The imagery available to a dramatist working in a less naturalistic framework is not available here. Thus, there is a tendency in naturalist plays for objects to be invested with a symbolic importance. For example, in *Look Back in Anger*, the church bells are always associated with the forces of convention in society, and they are opposed by the jazz trumpet Jimmy plays, which is associated with a free, natural human state of affairs unrestricted by convention and social pressure. As the play proceeds the audience is educated into a sense of this special meaning for these objects, so that, when the bells ring as Helena leaves in Act Three, the association serves to reinforce the significance of her action and to place it in the whole context of the dramatic meaning. This, in its turn, reinforces Helena's rejection of Jimmy a little earlier when she screams out at him to stop playing his trumpet in the next room.

Essential to the reading of dramatic language is a sense of what is not said. Remember that characters remain on stage when they are not speaking, and that the meaning of what is said is modified by the reactions of those characters who are not speaking. It is a useful technique to note on each page of the text who is present, and to ask oneself how they are reacting to the action. In *Look Back in Anger* this is particularly the case since Jimmy's speeches occupy so much of the dialogue. If we fail to visualise the reponses of the other characters we will underestimate the importance of their reactions in modifying the effect of Jimmy's rhetoric on the audience. Osborne is often quite explicit with stage directions in this respect; for instance, Cliff shakes his head and Alison leans against the board and closes her eyes. We should, however, be aware that the reaction of characters on a stage are not restricted to such specific gestures, and that Cliff and Alison may be significantly present even when they are not doing anything. Thus the lack of reaction they show to many of Jimmy's attacks in Act One can be used to indicate to the audience that they are inured to what is a very long-established pattern of behaviour, and can further establish the extent to which Jimmy's attacks are obsessional, returning time and time again to the same two or three main concerns—class, the inertia of Alison and Cliff, and his obsession with figures from the past whom he idealises.

The setting

To return for a moment to setting. There is a tendency for readers to think that the descriptions of scenes, or stage directions matter less than dialogue and so to skip over these when they read a play. Nothing could be further from the truth. The dialogue can be understood properly only when we have a clear visual sense of what is *happening* on the stage when it is spoken. Therefore, special attention should be paid to descriptions of setting, costume, stage directions and so on . . .. If we consider the way the setting and positioning of characters on stage in Act One parallel those of Act Three Scene One, we can see how significant such instructions from the author are. In the later scene the dress of the characters emphasises the parallel, with Helena now clad in an old shirt of Jimmy's just as Alison was in Act One. Much of the action that follows re-emphasises this parallel, so that we are able to see that the setting draws attention to the similarities of the situation. Of course, the irony resides in the fact that it quickly becomes clear that the relationship between Helena and Jimmy is much shallower than that between Jimmy and Alison, so that the parallel setting, costuming and stage grouping of characters serves to reinforce the differences between the two moments in the play. We can see that stage effects may be quite subtly employed to emphasise dramatic structure.

Recapitulation

(1) A play is more than words, and to read it properly you must continually seek to visualise the intended effects that the playwright wishes the actors to realise in a performance.

(2) All plays operate within certain rules or conventions. These are tacit or explicit agreements between the actors and the audience about what is or is not acceptable within the framework of the performance. To understand a play it is necessary to decide what these rules are, and to place the play within the context of theatre history to determine this.

(3) Visualising a play requires an awareness of reaction and interaction between all the characters on the stage and not just the character who is speaking.

(4) Setting and grouping of characters may serve to emphasise patterns within the dramatic structure which allow us to see the overall shape of the play's meaning.

Some specimen questions

(1) *Is Jimmy Porter a typical 'spokesman of his generation'?*

A good answer to this question would stress that many of Jimmy's attitudes were representative of a specific class and age group in the early 1950s. It would acknowledge the fact that *Look Back in Anger* is one of a number of literary works produced in the period which take up a broadly anti-Establishment* position. It would, however, draw attention to the fact that there are as many significant differences between the attitudes within this general category as there are similarities. It would, therefore, emphasise the need to treat the play as an individual work of art as well as a significant sociological and historical document. As a result, it would draw attention to the complexity of Jimmy's character. It would show that Jimmy is presented as a very individual figure whose problems are rooted in a complex psychological response to the past. It would emphasise the stress laid on the personal aspect of Jimmy's past. In addition it would point to the refusal of the play simply to state a *thesis* about the problems of post-war Britain.

Finally, the answer might indicate that Osborne has succeeded in creating a very complex, individual character whose personal failures and obsessions express many of the predominant concerns of his time. Thus, Jimmy's demand for a virile moral idealism is symptomatic of his awareness that the traditional structures and institutions have failed, and that nothing beyond a pragmatic and opportunistic vision has replaced them. The essentially pessimistic note on which the play ends is worth stressing, too, since it seems to indicate that Osborne identifies with Jimmy's sense of disillusion, and wishes to draw attention to the difficulties that the collapse of assured values has brought for the new young group of educated Britains who emerged in the post-war period.

---

(2) Look Back in Anger *fails as a play because it is finally only a series of obsessional dramatic monologues. Discuss.*

Clearly the play is dominated by the monologues of Jimmy Porter, though this is truer of Act One than it is of the later acts of the play. The question turns on the extent to which we believe that the other characters are realised in and through stage action. Alison certainly develops considerably as a character, and the need that she and Jimmy have for one another is clearly shown to affect Jimmy as much as her by the time we arrive at Act Three. Alison is certainly not a mere cipher. She makes several significant choices which shape the action of the play: first, when she chooses to leave; secondly, when she returns. Also, there is a significant choice, related in the play as past action, when she chooses to marry Jimmy. The scene with her father draws attention to the fact that Jimmy and she are in a relationship which has been created by the two of them. Whether we agree with him or not Osborne seems to be indicating here that Alison is partly guilty of 'sitting on the fence'. By the end of the play she and Jimmy are shown to be locked in a very complex personal relationship which has fundamentally altered both

*See the first footnote on p.9.

of them: Alison has been forced to accept the loss of her assured values, and Jimmy has been forced to face the cost in personal terms of his desire for an absolute commitment to honesty and moral openness.

Cliff is a character whose significance can easily be overlooked. His overt role, to act as a buffer between Jimmy and Alison, is seen to be partly a cover for his own deep personal need to establish a relationship. He is clearly unable to survive without other people, and yet finds it difficult to form relationships. He is a warm and affectionate person, but the indications of a deep insecurity are clearly delineated. His decision to leave in Act Three Scene One shows that he, too, has been changed in the course of the play. His leaving is a form of retreat, and yet we feel that as a result of his exposure to Jimmy and the others he has been made more conscious of the need to search for an effective identity for himself. In dramatic terms Cliff is one of the main figures in the play. It is through his often quite conscious reactions that much of the direction of the action is focused. His role is a clear example of the need to consider reaction to speeches as well as simply dialogue.

Helena and Colonel Redfern are less complex characters. Yet even they are shown to be integrated into the main choice which Jimmy's monologues pose: the choice of how to survive in a world whose values are in turmoil. Helena is a realist who survives by deliberately restricting the range of emotions she will allow to affect her. As a result she survives, but not without being diminished in the process. Colonel Redfern serves to emphasise that much of what Jimmy asserts has happened to the present—that it has lost its direction—is confirmed by the disillusionment which is felt by those who lived by the assured values of the past. His regret for those lost values subtly draws attention to the element of nostalgia in Jimmy's cry that there are 'no good brave causes left'.

Although the play centres on the speeches of Jimmy, and the questions they pose, the other characters serve to create a rich pattern of reactions which deepen the effect on the audience.

---

(3) *Does* Look Back in Anger *make a significant use of symbols to communicate its meaning?*

A question about the use of symbols in the play would need to begin by drawing attention to the limitations inherent in the naturalist play. It would point to the difficulties involved in showing inner emotion within the convention, and, conversely, to the limitations it places on making broad general statements about the philosophical and social implication of the action. The setting itself is symbolic in such a play. The choice of place, a flat in a small Midland town; the time of year and day; the weather; even the repetitive and domestic task of ironing which Alison is engaged in when the play opens, all serve to symbolise the dull, flat and purposeless nature of the way of living within which the three characters are trapped.

The use of overt symbols is also clearly part of the play's effect. The church bells are used time and time again to symbolise the hypocritical acceptance of the values of outdated institutions and moral systems. The jazz trumpet of Jimmy is opposed to this as a symbol of a possible freer and more human alternative (significantly Alison tells Helena that before he began to run the sweet-stall he had his own jazz-band and wishes to do so again). The game of squirrels and bears is developed by Act Three as a telling symbol of the essentially escapist nature of the relationship that has grown up between Jimmy and Alison. The final speeches of Jimmy introduce this symbol into the main body of the action when he comments on the loneliness of the bear following his own breath in the dark forest with no warm herd or pack to support him. It may be remarked, too, that both bears and squirrels hibernate to survive the winter, a symbolic hint that Alison and Jimmy can survive only by a form of retreat from the harshness of reality.

Thus, throughout the play the action is supported and informed by a network of symbolic allusions which draw attention to the dramatic patterns and deepen their social and philosophical implications. However, it should be realised that all such symbolic allusions are also integrated into the naturalistic surface of the action. In this way they deepen, but do not disrupt the realistic element of the play.

---

(4) *In* Look Back in Anger *Jimmy is more obsessed with the past than he is concerned with the future. Do you agree?*

The title of the play *Look Back in Anger* gives us the clearest clue to its form. Jimmy spends at least as much time looking back in anger at a past which he regrets, since it embodied moral certitude and idealism, as he does looking forward to a possible better future. It is this quality in the play which provides us with the clearest insights into Osborne's theme. This would seem to be that Jimmy is trapped between a past from which he cannot escape and a future which he cannot accept. There is a strongly nostalgic quality in much of his response. His vision of the future is often a dismissive one. For example, he sees the later part of the twentieth century as becoming dominated by a soulless, technological vision, an era he categorises as 'the American Age'. This leads to a certain confusion in Jimmy's response. Thus, he castigates Helena in Act Two Scene One for refusing to face up to 'the ugly problems of the twentieth century' and retreating into a vision of an idyllic rural past, and yet he too would often appear to be guilty of a similar retreat. His escapist fantasy with Alison reflects just this process, as does his obsession with the romanticised visions of working class solidarity that he associates with the inter-war period and the quixotic knight errantry of the Spanish Civil War.

This obsession with the past is reinforced by the relative sympathy and understanding the play shows to exist between Jimmy and Alison's father, Colonel Redfern. The two are linked closely together in Alison's comment when she says:

> You're hurt because everything is changed. Jimmy is hurt because everything is the same. And neither of you can face it. Something's gone wrong somewhere, hasn't it? (p.68)

The point, perhaps, is that what Jimmy regrets is the moral certainty which Colonel Redfern recalls. But it is a certainty which, as Alison clearly sees, has been lost in their own times.

Jimmy fails to make any very clear comment on how the future might be changed. It is this which Helena comments on in Act Three when she accuses him of being essentially 'futile'. Yet is there not a legitimate purpose in drawing attention to the feeling of loss and purposelessness which characterised so much of the response of the post-war period? Some early critics and reviewers referred to Jimmy Porter pejoratively as 'a Wolverhampton Hamlet'. It might be worth reflecting that no one accuses Hamlet of failure because Fortinbras, not he, finally puts Denmark back together again at the end of the play. In fact there is a sense of loss which the recovery of the limited but balanced compromise of Fortinbras cannot erase. Similarly, at the end of *Look Back in Anger* the sensible and reasonable choices of Helena, rooted in an acceptance of half-beliefs and half-truths, is a viable but unattractive alternative to the self-destructive plunge into despair which Alison and Jimmy are shown to embrace. In drama as in life we may be forced to be practical, but we do not always admire ourselves for what we become in the process. *Look Back in Anger* illustrates the essentially modern problem of a loss of certitude. In this sense it *is* as much concerned with the past as with the future. Osborne, as a writer, is clearly deeply involved with an idea of the past which is often romantic and occasionally sentimental. His patriotism, and his sense of the importance of traditions, which strengthens in later plays, is present as early as this first success. But in the overall dramatic context it seems to be effectively balanced by the genuine anguish which reinforces Jimmy Porter's attacks, and which finally allows us to view him, if not as an attractive figure, or even a very clear-sighted one, at least as a man who is driven by a genuine desire to render an account of himself in uncompromisingly human terms.

Part 5

Suggestions for further reading

The text

The only existing text is that first published in 1957 by Faber. There have been no significant emendations to the text since the first edition: John Osborne, *Look Back in Anger*, Faber and Faber, London, 1957

Other works by the author

John Osborne and Anthony Creighton: *Epitaph for George Dillon*, Faber and Faber, London, 1958; Criterion Books, London, 1958

The Entertainer, Faber and Faber, London, 1957; Criterion Books, London, 1958

The World of Paul Slickey, Faber and Faber, London, 1961

Luther, Faber and Faber, London, 1961; Criterion Books, London, 1961

A Subject of Scandal and Concern, Faber and Faber, London, 1961

Plays for England, Faber and Faber, London, 1963 (contains *Under Plain Cover* and *The Blood of the Bambergs*)

Tom Jones: a Screenplay, Faber and Faber, London, 1964; revised ed. Grove Press, New York, 1964

Inadmissable Evidence, Faber and Faber, London, 1965

A Patriot for Me, Faber and Faber, London, 1966

A Bond Honoured, Faber and Faber, London, 1966

Time Present, Faber and Faber, London, 1968

The Hotel in Amsterdam, Faber and Faber, London, 1968

Right Prospectus — a play for television, Faber and Faber, London, 1970

Naturalist Drama in Germany, Manchester University Press, Manchester, 1971

Very like a Whale, Faber and Faber, London, 1971

West of Suez, Faber and Faber, London, 1971

Gift of Friendship, Faber and Faber, London, 1972

A Place calling itself Rome, Faber and Faber, London, 1973

Watch it Come Down, Faber and Faber, London, 1975

The End of Me Old Cigar and *Jack and Jill* (Two plays), Faber and Faber, London, 1975

General reading

TRUSSLER, SIMON: *The Plays of John Osborne: an Assessment*, Gollancz, London, 1969

TRUSSLER, SIMON: *John Osborne* (Writers and Their Work No. 213), Longmans, London, 1969

HAYMAN, RONALD: *John Osborne* (Contemporary Playwrights), Heinemann, London, 1968

BANHAM, MARTIN: *Osborne* (Writers and Critics), Oliver and Boyd, Edinburgh, 1969

ALLSOP, KENNETH: *The Angry Decade*, Peter and Owen, London, 1958

GASCOIGNE, BAMBER: *Twentieth Century Drama*, Hutchinson, London, 1962

RUSSELL TAYLOR, JOHN: *Anger and After*, Methuen, London, 1962; revised ed. Penguin Pelican Books, Harmondsworth, 1963

RUSSELL TAYLOR, JOHN, (ED.): *John Osborne: Look Back in Anger* (Macmillan Casebook Series), Macmillan, London, 1968

The author of these notes

GARETH GRIFFITHS was educated at the University of Wales. Subsequently he taught at the University of East Anglia, the University of Missouri and Macquarie University, Sydney, Australia, where he is currently Senior Lecturer in Drama.

He is the author of *A Double Exile: African and West Indian Writing Between Two Cultures*, 1978. He has published articles on modern drama and African literature in European and American journals.